TAMASHIWARI

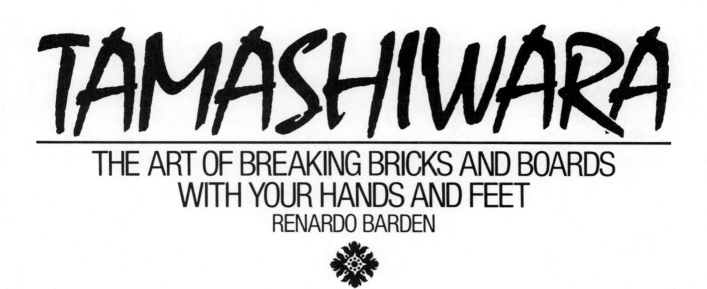

TAMASHIWARA

THE ART OF BREAKING BRICKS AND BOARDS WITH YOUR HANDS AND FEET

RENARDO BARDEN

CONTEMPORARY
BOOKS, INC.
CHICAGO

Library of Congress Cataloging-in-Publication Data

Barden, Renardo.
    Tamashiwara: the art of breaking bricks and
boards with your hands and feet.

    Includes index
    1. Karate.   I. Title.
GV1114.3.B36   1985   793′8′153   85-22353
ISBN 0-8092-5186-8 (pbk.)

Copyright © 1985 by Renardo Barden
All rights reserved
Published by Contemporary Books, Inc.
180 North Michigan Avenue, Chicago, Illinois 60601
Manufactured in the United States of America
Library of Congress Catalog Card Number:
International Standard Book Number: 0-8092-5186-8

Published simultaneously in Canada by Beaverbooks, Ltd.
195 Allstate Parkway, Valleywood Business Park
Markham, Ontario L3R 4T8 Canada

CONTENTS

She has taught by example: for encouraging both Oogahwompah and me to keep improvising, this book is for my mother.

TAMASHIWARA

If the formal exercises and the practice fighting we have seen up till this point are the parents of karate, the stone-breaking techniques are the child. The basic formal exercises without the stone-breaking techniques are like a chestnut tree that bears no nuts.

This Is Karate, by Mas Oyama

Boards don't hit back.

Bruce Lee

ACKNOWLEDGMENTS

First of all, I would like to thank Mito Uyehara, an unflinching individualist who provided me with legitimate opportunities and the sometimes acrid challenges I met as well as I could.

Geri Simon saved me from walking the plank a time or two and did what she could, within the limits of her position, to be a friend.

With regard to this book, for contributions and conversations, all of which were above and beyond the call of either duty or friendship, I'd like to thank Don Baird, Hee Il Cho, Ed Brown, Dave Lowry, Joko Ninomiya, Richard Vera, Paul Maslak, and Tom Bloom. Scott Dinger took a helpful interest and would have helped with modeling except for the cast on his arm. George Chung and Cindi Rothrock were kind and willing and would have had more photographic input except for pressing schedules and deadlines. Shihan Tak Kubota was a model of good humor and patience and generously made himself available for several photo sessions and conversations despite the demands of his hectic schedule.

I thank as well the many martial artists who've shared their time and ideas with me over a period of several years. The best of this book may actually accurately represent their experiences, viewpoints, and insights, while the worst will surely reflect my own shortcomings, including those that are probably inevitable in coming from one who is neither a breaking expert nor even a reasonably diligent martial artist.

Tarin Dhaisantah provided almost all and certainly the best photographs appearing herein and proved very patient when it came to trying to explain a few rudiments to a rather inept pupil.

Rohana, Michael, Mary, and Chris were patient when I was preoccupied with book details, and Nancy Crossman and Clay Smudsky were patient when I was perhaps more preoccupied than they might have hoped.

INTRODUCTION

Why breaking? Well, hundreds of years ago, the Japanese samurai tested the quality of their new sword blades on peasants and criminals. As this culture came to be modified and softened, swords were tested on bundles of damp straw or bamboo clusters. Similarly, it is perhaps accurate to speculate that those early traditional masters of the fighting arts proved the effectiveness of their techniques on fellow combatants. Indeed, there are theories that the eccentric fashion in which many old-style karate techniques are executed stems from the construction of the armor worn by warriors of the time. Slightly more contemporary tales of the early Okinawan karate masters would likewise tend to indicate that first-rate technique could indeed be employed against a variety of knaves and challengers.

While it wouldn't be quite accurate to claim that modern men are either less warlike or kinder to their enemies, it is certainly true that modern weapons have radically altered human conflict. Tanks have supplanted the horse, automatic weaponry the sword, and nearly everywhere on our streets, handguns or sawed-off shotguns have replaced the fist. Breaking has

therefore become a method of self-testing whereby the martial arts adept can assess the nature and extent of empty-handed fighting skills without injuring an opponent.

Many years before I became involved in the martial arts, a friend took me to see Akiro Kurosawa's *The Seven Samurai,* the Japanese movie and model for the highly vaunted American Western movie, John Sturges's *The Magnificent Seven.*

The Kurosawa film takes up the plight of a village that has been terrorized by brigands for many years. With every harvest the village crops are expropriated by bandits, leaving the peasants with only enough food to survive until the next harvest. As the movie opens, the village patriarch sends three representatives out to recruit some samurai to fight the brigands. Since the town is too poor to pay its defenders anything but room and board, the villagers are instructed to "look for hungry samurai."

As part of the process of selection, a visit is paid to the scene of a practice fencing match between two samurai who are using the wooden *bokken,* or Japanese training swords. One of the duelists clearly has it all over the other, defeating him handily then withdrawing with grave modesty. Embarrassed by the presence of the crowd, the defeated swordsman becomes furious and insists on a rematch—with real blades. Reluctantly, the winner vanquishes his opponent, this time with fatal consequences. Then and there I became a fan of the martial arts; I suppose I like the noble samurai who killed with such artistic stoicism. I felt especially drawn to the idea of a world where brutality could be held in check by gamesmanship and honor. Had the defeated swordsman only been willing to accept his defeat, he would have been able to live and, perhaps, improve as a martial artist.

Years later, scenes from this movie again came to mind when I witnessed my first breaking demonstration in the martial arts. My companions, not themselves martial artists, considered the black belts who were about to snap boards and pulverize piles of cinder blocks as so many fanatics whose enthusiasm for karate had made them eager to risk pain and broken bones for the ego gratification of impressing an audience.

I'd like to report that my friends were converted and that the breaks were 100-percent successful, injury-free, and dramatic, even awe-inspiring. Some of the breaks, however, just didn't happen. And in a few other cases, the would-be breaker tried over and over again to break his material—whether it was wood, brick, tile, or ice. In one instance, there was what we thought of as the unmistakable sound of breaking finger bones. My non–martial arts friends found this barbaric and even thought differently of me later for not sharing their wholly negative view.

Perhaps it had to do with the fencing match in *The Seven Samurai.* The losing swordsman was convinced he'd won the match, and just before he received his fatal wound was demanding proof that there was something more to his many years of training than a mere game to be determined by a majority of public opinion. In comparing this losing fencer with the black belts trying to pound cinder blocks into dust storms, I realized that they too were under pressure, intent upon finding out how real was all the theory and training to which they had devoted themselves. Either karate training would enable an expert to kill or disable with one punch or it wouldn't. Either their training had begun to reward them

with these skills or it hadn't. They had the good sense (or morality) not to try to damage people; therefore, even after allowing for some measure of egotism, the breaking demonstration was at least partly a willingness to make real and undeniable skills (or failures) a matter of public record. I argued to my non-martial arts companions that, however foolhardy and exhibitionistic the demonstrations, this willingness to risk buffoonery in front of a crowd did demand a kind of courage.

There were some successful breaks that night, and I concluded afterward that the injuries and broken bones that did occur were probably the result of inadequate preparation. Slightly better-informed conversations held years later with many of the most experienced and talented breakers in the United States tended to confirm that opinion.

"You must have a lot of self-confidence and keep your mind completely free from doubt," says Santa Monica, California, Tae Kwon Do master Hee Il Cho. "Otherwise you're going to injure yourself badly. You don't hit what you're going to break until your mind is already sure."

Many years prior to this conversation, the male half of my sixth grade class was utterly convinced that karate and judo black belts had to register their hands with the police. In our young imaginations these superhuman warriors had to carry special cards around in their wallets. These "business" cards, as I remember the fantasy, had to be shown before a karate expert could be legally entitled to shatter bones and end lives. The expert's hands were said to be as hard as iron. According to our imaginings, the target of any slight slap would be, at the least, crippled for life. The Asian martial arts were new to the United States and highly exotic. As kids, we were only too ready to embellish the wildest of such tales and superstitions. Luckily, there were no pseudoexperts around to give us bad advice. If there had been, we might have been only too willing to go out and subject our young limbs to the pain that is always visited on the restless and impatient.

Although with proper supervision most kids aged 10 and up can safely break, say, a single dried pine board, serious breaking and body-toughening procedures are not for young limbs or beginning martial artists. Indulging in rigor-

There are no champion children breakers. Their bones are too fragile and too easily injured for them to begin conditioning their bodies for the trauma of breaking. Though children somewhat older and more experienced than these are often eager to try breaking, they must start with very easy surfaces and be supervised carefully.

ous hand and foot conditioning before you reach physical maturity is both foolish and dangerous. Driving a car, fishing, making love, walking a tightrope, swimming, and breaking bricks with hands and feet are only a few human skills not likely to be mastered by simple reading of a book. This is not, of course, to devalue books on such topics. On the contrary, they can be quite informative and useful to readers prepared to distinguish among the needs for information, inspiration, and hands-on instruction. There are certain omissions in this book which are quite deliberate. Never mind that there are a multitude of effective styles and methods of instruction: the clear message here is that any reader who needs rudimentary explanations of how to make a fist or assume a basic stance is not prepared to break in the first place. If you are a beginning martial artist you need a mastery of your art's basics before you can make the best use of these materials. And if you are an advanced martial artist, you are undoubtedly already familiar with certain basics and are ready to pay atten-

tion to the finer details that can make a difference to your ability to deliver breaking power.

Likewise, there are countless martial arts books which come complete with extensive stretching programs and warm-up exercises. Once again, the attempt is to be selective rather than exhaustive. In this, I hope to address what may be the most common complaint of serious martial artists about books on the martial arts—that they are swollen with an excess of information about stretching and warm-ups (easily available from other sources) and a dearth of detail with respect to the martial art(s) actually being written about. These serious and experienced martial artists will also tell you a thing or two about injuries: for one thing they are most often the afflictions of the ill-prepared. Young people and beginners flushed with enthusiasm, because they are inclined to be both ambitious and hasty, are often both ill-prepared and needlessly injured. So be warned. Take your time and spare yourself some doctor's bills and many hours of pain and setback.

1
THE INNER FORCES: KI AND CHI

Throughout recorded history there have been wide differences of opinion concerning all religious, spiritual, and speculative matters. No sooner does a mystic or seer come along to declare that there is a God or some reality higher than the everyday reality people believe they share with each other, than someone arrives on the scene to debunk such an assertion. These days, if you polled a cross section of Americans about their belief in the existence of God, you would naturally expect to find some differences of opinion. Likewise, if you polled a cross section of martial artists about the existence of *ki* or *chi* power, you would get another wide split.

Even black belts who are experienced breakers reveal a seeming lack of agreement on the *ki/chi* power issue. Some claim that this inner force enables them to experience an extra surge of power. Others, equally expert, assert flat out that they've never experienced such a thing and even deny the existence of such an energy.

KI POWER: FACT OR FANTASY?

In the days when the Asian martial arts were relatively unknown in the West, the powerful punching and kicking techniques executed by the various masters were considered something quite out of the ordinary. More often than not, the early breaking masters believed and explained that their extraordinary physical prowess came from the development of some mystical essence whose source was deep within themselves. In the Japanese-related arts, such a force came to be known as *ki*.

This mystical power and force was naturally awakened and developed, instructors explained to their students, through many years of devotion to the martial art being studied. First, however, it was assumed that the student had to develop a rudimentary physical mastery of the basic techniques of that art. Only after having developed these basic skills to near perfection was the student expected to begin to notice the more subtle mental and spiritual aspects of the arts.

The growth of this inner power was said to be stimulated by various breathing and meditation exercises introduced by the teachers. Restless students who complained of feeling nothing whatever were usually told it was just a matter of time. Gradually, partly in response to the impatience of the students and the increased competition for good students, instructors have tended to decrease or drop altogether these aspects of martial arts training.

The *ki* power debate is really probably just an extension of the original dispute. Is there absolute truth, an immortal soul, a God? Is there life after death? Is there a mystical internal power that the martial artist can come to acquire and nurture that can then help him develop in the martial arts?

Unhappily, such absolute questions are not easily answered, and while some people believe they have found the answers to these kinds of questions, the answers tend to be personal and will not often satisfy everyone. If the question cannot be answered, however, there are perhaps a couple of observations that might be made about the *ki* power issue in general.

Martial artists who believe in the existence of *ki* power do tend to agree that it is an energy that develops over time in response to training—that its growth depends on increasing physical proficiency. If that is in fact the case, the skeptic presumably has only to continue to perfect martial arts skills in order to become aware of *ki.*

Also, as there are a great many highly skilled breakers who do not believe in *ki,* one can be assured that breaking skills are something that can be perfected without adopting an artificial belief in *ki* power.

But finally, and perhaps most importantly, breakers who believe in *ki* power unite with breakers who do not in asserting that abundant *ki* power will not enable the physically unprepared martial artist to break. Nor, agree the experts, will this spiritualizing force protect the student from suffering injuries identical to those suffered by unconditioned unbelievers.

The fact is that, both in and out of the martial arts, many people have extolled the benefits of deep breathing, meditation, or yoga. And, if meditation does produce a calm mind, then there is an obvious compatibility between meditation and training to break in the martial arts. For if there's one thing that all expert breakers agree on, it is that doubt, the slightest shadow of uncertainty in the mind, will prevent the breaker from successfully breaking his materials.

If meditation, *tai chi,* visualization, or some other form of quieting exercise can stimulate

Strength and concentration take precedence over *ki* power in Takayuki Kubota's training.

calmness, concentration, and confidence, then perhaps it is best to adopt a moderate philosophical attitude toward the existence of *ki* power. Whether or not these things will nurture your *ki,* perhaps you should merely ask youself if in your daily life you could benefit from being calmer and more self-confident. If so, then perhaps you'll open your mind and take a few minutes to experiment.

CHI

The so-called soft styles or Chinese martial arts also identify an inner force, the cultivation of which is considered important to the martial artist.

The word *chi* to the Chinese means the energy contained in the air. Mist, wind, breath, and air as well as human beings are said to contain *chi.* Many in the Chinese arts believe that *chi* is an inner current that pulses through the body along with the circulation of the blood.

The Chinese, however, do not think of this mysterious inner force purely in terms of the power it can contribute to martial arts techniques. Though it is believed to have definite destructive potentials, *chi* is also thought to be the source of physical and spiritual health.

According to Chinese modes of thought, the *chi* energy flows through the body along certain physical pathways known as *meridians*. These meridians, which have been the subject of a great deal of study for thousands of years, form the basis of Chinese acupuncture and much traditional medicine. In a martial sense, certain of these meridians are considered to be so sensitive that strikes to them are likely to result in death. Like much else in Chinese martial arts, perhaps for good reason, these lethal points are considered secret.

In the Chinese martial arts, practitioners seek not just perfect and powerful technique, but a way of movement that will stimulate the development and flow of *chi* along these meridians within the practitioner. Since *chi* does not, according to Chinese thought, automatically produce physical power in the martial artist, Chinese kung fu experts with an interest in developing the power to break often undertake various other areas of physical study, including the toughening methods that can be practiced on wooden dummies as well as the esoteric iron palm training that will be discussed later in this book.

2
MENTAL PREPARATION

Master Hee Il Cho, a Tae Kwon Do karate master based in Santa Monica, California, is renowned for his impressive breaking skills. While the ability to break boards and bricks held or supported on a pedestal is not that uncommon, few these days are capable of using punches and kicks to break boards thrown in the air. Such breaks require not only sharply focused blows but also extraordinary eye and hand coordination, perfect timing, and a high rate of speed; hence, they are commonly called *speed breaks*. The Korean-born Hee Il Cho seems to enjoy something of a monopoly on this type of break.

DEALING WITH FEARS

Not surprisingly, he has a psychological attitude that he seems to share with many of the best breakers in the country. Like others who have developed high levels of breaking skills, Cho believes that pain and fear are obstacles that must be confronted, experienced, and finally surmounted by anyone who wants to become a complete martial artist. This is not a teaching philosophy Cho enforces with ferocity, in the

Taekwon-do master Hee Il Cho executes an outside crescent kick, one of the many kicks he uses to break with.

5

Hee Il Cho breaks first the lower of two boards with a hook kick. Without touching his leg to the floor, Cho then proceeds to break the second board.

way that a traditional master of the martial arts might. Instead it is a teaching philosophy implemented with a kind of simple persistence. Cho once recounted the following conversation.

"Master, do I have to fight? I just can't. It's not part of my nature. I might get hurt."

"Yes, you have to fight."

"Why?"

"Because I want you to know that fear you have inside yourself, that fear that makes you so sure you can't face an opponent. I want you to fight here in the studio, protected by the safety of the equipment. When I see you and know why you have that fear—where it came from—I will talk to you again. Together we can erase that fear."

In the martial arts one student's fears are often quite like another's. While some students are afraid of looking foolish in front of their peers, others are afraid they will be hit and hurt. Still others are afraid of injuring their partners. Likewise, not a few students are afraid of striking anything hard with either hand or foot. In fact, this fear may be the strongest dread that students who are inexperienced as fighters have to confront.

Fear of Breaking

The two most common fears with respect to breaking are probably the fear of being embarrassed in the event of failure and the fear of incurring injury.

The first step in dealing with your fears with regard to breaking is to acknowledge them as being reasonable. If you've never hit anything harder than a speed bag in your life, and you don't know how to punch properly, your fears are quite reasonable. In such a case, the thing to do to overcome those fears is to prepare yourself, first by acquiring punching skills, second by getting yourself into reasonably good physical condition, and finally by learning to strike increasingly harder surfaces, gradually and carefully.

In fact, gradualism is the key to the mastery of any fear in the martial arts. The only problem with the practice of this kind of gradualism is that it requires a measure of honesty. You must be brave enough to be honest with yourself in front of others. You must be willing to start at a level within reach of your own body and spirit and then proceed from there. The initial courage and honesty are essential; otherwise, you will only be making things difficult, establishing for yourself a pattern of injury and failure.

SELF-CONFIDENCE

Long ago, there were two young lovers who lived in the forest. One day the girl was attacked by a man-eating tiger. Though her lover arrived in time to frighten the animal away, there was little he could do to treat her injuries. After a short struggle for life, the girl died.

Naturally, her young husband was exceedingly sorrowful and angry. At one point, in fact, he determined to avenge himself on the tiger. He took to the jungle armed only with a bow and arrow. For several days he trailed the tiger and then, one afternoon, seeing the form of a sleeping tiger, let fly with a single arrow. The arrow sank very deeply into its target, but the tiger did not so much as growl or twitch. In fact, on going forward to investigate, the young man saw that his arrow had pierced a heavy stone covered with shadows in the pattern of a tiger's stripes. This story, of course, made the young man quite famous. He became known far and wide as the archer so powerful that he could shoot an arrow through stone. Unfortunately, he never managed to duplicate the feat again. Initially, he had been consumed by rage and intensity and had no doubt about his ability to kill the hated tiger with a single arrow. The power of his intention gave him confidence and enabled him to embed the arrow into a rock.

This story, illustrative of the importance of self-confidence and a doubt-free mind, is said to have given rise to a Japanese saying: "A strong will can pierce a stone." This is the story told by Master Otake of the *Tenshin Shoden Katori Shinto Ryu* school of swordsmanship and recorded in William Scott Wilson's translation of *Hagakure, The Book of the Samurai.*

Pu Gill Gwon, a Tae Kwon Do master with a fondness for breaking the tops off whiskey bottles and leaving the beverage therein, believes not only that confidence is indispensable to the breaker, but that breaking itself can help martial artists *build* self-confidence.

"Breaking techniques develop confidence. Properly done, you will know just how effective your strikes are. You will know that if a target had been a point on an opponent's body you would have shattered it," Gwon has said.

EGO

There are countless stories concerning those whose inflated sense of self-worth has gotten them into trouble and martial artists who wish to try breaking should avoid crossing the fine line between self-confidence and egotism.

From the *Hagakure* comes the story of Shimomura Shoun. It seems that Lord Naoshige was bragging about the physical prowess of a youth named Katsushige, explaining to Shoun that Katsushige could outwrestle those who were older. Shoun replied that he himself was the best at seated wrestling. At that point, he jerked up Katsushige and threw him viciously onto the floor. Mincing no words, Shoun spoke to Katsushige. "To be prideful about your strength while your mettle is not yet established is likely to bring you shame in the midst of people. You are weaker than you look." Then Shoun withdrew.

The ego creates many modern martial arts problems, some of them funnier than others.

Several years ago, internationally renowned kickboxing champion Benny Urquidez was invited to give a full-contact seminar at a tournament in San Jose, California. That evening, Urquidez agreed to give the audience a little fighting demonstration. A black belt from the area volunteered to spar with Urquidez, and the "match" began without much ceremony. Urquidez came out typically relaxed, exuding the informed self-confidence that his undefeated record as a fighter had given him. He began to get the "feel" of his opponent's fighting style. Having proved himself consistently against all comers, Urquidez simply came out willing to hit and kick with moderate force against an opponent whose skill levels were unknown to him. He was just giving an exhibition of his skills. His opponent, however, felt he had something to prove and was soon hitting Benny harder than Benny was hitting him, making himself look good at the champ's expense. Urquidez seemed willing to accept that his opponent felt he'd been given an irresistible opportunity to test his skills against the best and simply adjusted by fighting a little harder. This only seemed to add fuel to his opponent's attack. In fact, the newcomer managed to sweep Benny off his feet. A few people in the audience hooted their approval, wondering if the world champ was destined to meet his match in an exhibition bout. Those of us who'd seen Urquidez in action merely shook our heads.

Urquidez got to his feet, smiled to his opponent, signaling him that he hadn't been hurt and that, moreover, he didn't begrudge his opponent the right to sweep him if he could. This changed the nature of the exhibition, though. With no show of anger or impatience, Urquidez simply began to hit his opponent harder to the body. In short order the challenger's fight was hammered out of him, and he soon found it all he could do to stay on his feet. At this point, Benny couldn't resist a couple of smiling gestures, inviting his opponent to continue the match. The challenger, however, was ready to stop. After all, it was only an exhibition match, wasn't it?

Nor was that the last instance of swollen ego experienced in San Jose that night. After the tournament a group of perhaps 20 black belts went to eat at a downtown steak house. Though they were sitting in the restaurant section at a long table, several, including Urquidez, had a view of the goings-on in the bar next door. At one point there was some excitement. It seems that some of the bar's patrons (not apparently connected with the martial arts) were in a fighting mood and had stepped outside. As it turned out, one man was pounding on another man. A third man, also from the bar, intervened and received for his trouble a similar pounding from the belligerent. There was some talk among the martial artists watching through the window about going out to break it up. But before any such idea took hold, the two defeated fighters took off up the street. The "victorious" fighter got up and came back into the bar. As he did, he looked into the restaurant area where, among the nearest black belt spectators were Benny Urquidez and current PKA Heavyweight Champion, six-foot seven-inch Big John Jackson. "What are you looking at?" the drunken brawler growled, addressing all 20 black belts, but glaring especially at Urquidez who was nearest to him. "You guys want some of what they got?" I remember the grin that came over Urquidez's face and the burst of laughter that came from the

rest of us. "No, man," Benny said. "I just want to sit down and finish eating my food."

The drunk must have had a rational thought or two after that because he disappeared in a hurry. The group of black belts were paying their tab when the police (called by the bartender) arrived. Though the drunken "winner" had long since made himself scarce, on the way back to the hotel, John Jackson and some of his companions passed the "losers." Sure enough, they were headed back to the bar for another go at their enemy. Since Jackson and friends knew that cops were waiting inside the door, they laughed to think that these two with their torn shirts and bloodied noses were about to lose something other than pride, shirt buttons, and blood trickles—their freedom. John Jackson, then a full-contact contender and bouncer in his hometown of Gary, Indiana, laughed all the way to his hotel room.

The point behind all this is that the ego delights in creating conditions that are dangerous to the physical and mental health of the martial artist. No matter how much you believe in mind over matter, and no matter how careful you are to remove all doubt and fear of failure from your mind, if your opponent has done the same thing more effectively than you have, you are going to suffer defeat.

In a breaking situation, of course, the defeat you suffer will come from the inertness of your materials, their refusal to break in response to your techniques. You can, as some have done, persist in hitting or kicking your materials until the bones break. And if you're really dedicated, you can persist beyond that. For the sake of demonstrating how thoroughly you've mastered the aspects of indomitability, you can disable yourself for weeks, months, or years.

Granted, determination and unwillingness to concede defeat will go a long way toward creating the mental set you need to become a successful breaker. Only you can decide how far is too far (as long as you're deciding only for yourself). Therefore, a long time before you set up your materials in front of a group of people, you should have made some decisions. Admittedly, you don't want to have a shadow of doubt fall over your mind as you're standing there preparing your break. So you need to do some serious thinking beforehand. Remembering that, whatever else you think you're doing, you're providing spectacle and entertainment for an audience who will be indifferent to your medical expenses and pain, you will need to set your own limits in advance and adhere to them.

DO YOU BELIEVE IN MAGIC?

Jason Randal, a black belt in Tang Soo Do karate and judo, specializes in card tricks and sleight-of-hand magic. Aside from being a professional magician and a martial artist, Randal is a Hollywood stuntman. In each field, he applies what he knows about human blind spots to his magic shows, stunt work, and the martial arts. Randal has some sound thoughts on the difference between what people seem to be doing and what they are actually doing. Like all magicians, he is a specialist in creating certain kinds of confusions. An otherwise skilled martial artist could certainly learn a great deal from talking with Jason Randal. Nonetheless, as a serious martial artist, Randal doesn't confuse the appearances he creates in magic shows for the martial arts. And he doesn't profess to be a world champion breaker.

On the other hand, many in the martial arts have more to offer in the way of showmanship, magic, and theatrics than legitimately acquired and *sustained* skills. More troublesome are those people with legitimate skills who choose hocus-pocus over the martial arts. They rationalize, of course, that they are promoting the arts to an indifferent and unappreciative public and are therefore entitled to a modicum of charlatanism. Invariably, people like this give themselves high ranks (because everybody else does) and the martial arts a bad name.

One martial artist who had allegedly taped a show for the television program "That's Incredible" was apparently excised from a recent pro-gram. The story was that he was going to use *ki* power to walk over a carpet of eggs. This was something the high-ranking black belt was able to do. Unhappily, it was something the production staff of "That's Incredible" were able to do, too. No, nobody cooked any omelets. It seems the eggs were made of durable plastic!

Just as a circus is a mix of really extraordinary talent and hoopla, so the martial arts has its equivalent talking horses and dogs who are experts in math. They are 10th degree black belts who set things on fire. They lie on beds of nails and have cinder blocks hammered to powder on their chests. They wear see-through blindfolds and cut apples and watermelons with samurai swords, sparing the human flesh on which the fruits are positioned. They make themselves fabulous costumes and take fantastic titles for themselves. And they are in fact demonstrating themselves and not the martial arts.

Frankly, reasonably sophisticated martial artists are the hardest audience to please. I remember several years ago seeing a martial artist execute a reasonably good *kata* at a tournament in the Midwest. He had, however, made an unfortunate decision to do this while wearing a ninja costume, complete with mask. The five *kata* judges seemed to me to score him lower than they had scored competitors whose *kata* were less impressive. The would-be ninja was simply trying to impress the wrong audience. The five karate judges actually penalized him for introducing a costume they thought was entirely superfluous to competitive martial arts. Other demonstrators have made the same mistake. They may have wowed the non–martial arts segment of their audience, but they definitely diminished themselves before their peers. Once lost, this peer respect is impossible to regain fully. The non-martial arts audience will forget you within minutes after your dazzling performance, but your colleagues will never forgive you for pretending to skills you don't have.

3
DEALING WITH PAIN

A few words about pain are in order.

For one thing, we all have to experience some. For another, a few people profess to enjoy it (at least in small quantities). And, perhaps more importantly, those who have experienced the nitty-gritty of human conflict tend to look at pain a bit differently from most of us.

"Consider it this way," says Ed Brown, one of the breakers profiled in Chapter 9. "Somebody might grab you and apply excruciating pain until you pass out. The first time it's not going to take too much to get you to pass out. The second time you're going to be able to hold out a little longer. The third time, still longer. You see, if you can learn to tolerate pain, increase your threshold of pain, you're going to have an upper hand on the person who's attacking you."

World Champion Benny Urquidez, though he's made his livelihood from giving more pain than he receives, would agree, at least in part. Urquidez, who may well be the best kickboxing fighter of all time, and is quite probably the best American full-contact fighter of all time, has never to the author's knowledge gone in for breaking demonstrations. Yet he knows things about pain that most people never will.

Several years ago, Urquidez fought a Japanese kickboxer named Shinobu Onuki in Las Vegas. In the opening seconds of the very first round Onuki hit Urquidez flush on the jaw with a full-power roundhouse kick. The kick would have ended 99 out of 100 fights then and there. It had timing, focus, snap. Urquidez never saw it. But he took it and then smiled. In fact, he nodded an acknowledgment to his opponent and, as he did so, received the same technique on the other side of his face, just as hard. Again Urquidez smiled. This time, however, he managed to counter with a hook to the body. And, as though he'd just heard a funny joke, he still smiled as he delivered his punch. In the sixth round Urquidez knocked Onuki out with another left hook to the body. In grinning and fighting through that first round, Benny had followed what he called one of his five rules of fighting—never let your opponent know that you're in pain.

Consider the football cliche that nothing of significance is ever achieved without pain—no pain, no gain. That statement is a little too sweeping and simplistic, even when it is limited to a purely physical world. In fact, every sport has its mental dimension, and in a scientific sense, nothing could be further from the truth. Even in an athletic sense, brute force and a willingness to experience high doses of pain often seems like an unnecessary glorification of suffering, one that persists at least partly because of inadequate understanding of the task at hand. For just as various scientific breakthoughs, from the discovery of gravity to broadcasting and radioactivity, come about as a result of experimentation, so, on a more mundane level, do martial arts training insights; the truly prepared can minimize their pain, partly through experimentation.

How is pain related to preparedness? In a martial arts sense, there sometimes seems to be an almost inverse relationship. In this respect, I think of formerly nationally rated tournament fighter Larry Kelley. While other competitors often partied late into the night before a tournament, Kelley typically turned in early. Before coming to the tournament, Kelley spent considerable time stretching before fighting. He kept his mind on his goals and trained like a professional athlete. And while Kelley became one of the winningest light heavyweight tournament fighters in the country—never mind that he was and is one of the best kickers in the business—the thing that impressed observers about Kelley was that he never seemed to get injured. Tournament black belts fight hard, and injuries—most of them relatively minor—are quite common. Thus, while many fighters had to miss certain events due to various injuries, Kelley was always something of an iron man. Injuries never seemed to prevent Kelley from competing in tournaments. Because he was willing to experience the controlled pain of hard training, he was able to compete and experiment a great deal. Hence, the pain of training leads to preparedness; the preparedness leads to the opportunity to experiment; the experimentation leads to success.

In breaking, we are, of course, discussing a different martial arts application. We are also talking about an aspect of the martial arts that is more commonly associated with pain than any other. If you're seriously interested in breaking, there are a couple of kinds of pain you have to think about.

First of all, I know of no masters of breaking who believe you can achieve even competence in breaking on the basis of *chi* or *ki* power alone.

Indeed, while breaking may have the sort of spiritual dimension often ascribed to it, without adequate physical preparedness you'll never know.

Shihan Takayuki Kubota's attitude is typical of breakers. "If you think you're going to break boards and bricks with *ki* power alone," he laughs, "first you will have to break some bones." Then he puts on a mock face of pain and sorrow and mimes holding one arm up in a sling.

Other masters of breaking are less funny but equally emphatic. "You have to prepare for this type of thing over a long period of time," says Hee Il Cho, famous for his speed breaks.

To become good at breaking, you need to (1) have the patience to persist over the months and years of conditioning required (and for maintenance purposes, persist with your conditioning once you've acquired the skills) and (2) experience sufficient discomfort and, yes, pain, to gradually raise your pain tolerance to comparitively high levels.

Ideally, the martial artist could create a training program that involves only progressive levels of discomfort, ascending so gradually to a high level of breaking skill that the pain never becomes noticeable. Now, while this book will attempt to provide information and training ideas to help you develop just such a program, it's doubtful that you will always be able to remain comfortably within the very slow and gradual confines of your own approach. Sooner or later, you're going to push yourself, overdo,

Many martial artists use weights in their training, though few put them to the same uses as Kubota.

As illustrated by his stance, Tak Kubota teaches a supremely practical style of karate. His years of work with the Tokyo and Los Angeles police departments has made him impatient with highly theoretical karate.

and experience pain—sooner and more if you're impatient, later and less if you're willing to take it day by day.

However you manage to progress, you will be developing an increasing tolerance for pain, experiencing it more and accepting its messages. If you have the patience to persist in training despite a certain amount of pain, you will be rewarded by acquiring breaking skills at the fastest possible rate. On the other hand, if you're impatient, you'll be slowing yourself down by traveling sporadically between one reckless injury and the next. And it's possible you'll never arrive at success.

INCREASING YOUR PAIN TOLERANCE

There are as many ways of dealing with pain as there are people willing to confront it.

Dan DiVito, an eclectic Los Angeles Tae Kwon Do teacher, has made himself something of an expert in these matters. An avid fitness buff, DiVito derives great pleasure from training and enjoys as well almost any opportunity to free-spar with opponents who enjoy rigorous physical contact. As a teacher, DiVito believes it is important to prepare his students for the painful physical contact that is the essence of any self-defense encounter. To bring a student from a position of fear toward a tolerance of harder contact, DiVito has created a series of drills.

One exercise calls for partners to spar in slow motion, withholding all force save the lightest touch at first, then gradually, and with the permission of the partner, speeding up and adding small increments of force to each technique. Another drill with similar intent calls for one partner to execute "very light" techniques against the other. The target of these techniques practices rotating, twisting, backstepping, shifting weight, and turning the head in order to rob kicks and blows of their power. "It's very important," DiVito has said, "that the student learn to monitor attacks, that he learn to look at the kicks and punches coming toward him." Gradually, again with the permission of the partner, the blows are stiffened. Full-contact fighters, martial artists with a very real need for high pain tolerance levels, practice variations of this last DiVito drill, with particular emphasis on the abdominal area.

PKA World Middleweight Champion Jean Yves Theriault once included a particularly brutal form of abdominal conditioning in his training regimen. With a partner on a stepladder or standing over him, Theriault would abdominally absorb the shock of a falling 20-pound medicine ball. This practice was eventually given up, not because it was too hard on the abdominal area, but because as an exercise it endangered the champ's lower back. The exercise hasn't been given up altogether. These days, Theriault merely absorbs the same shock in an upright position.

As far as breaking is concerned, Tae Kwon Do master Pu Gill Gwon prepares himself for breaking by hitting his hands or feet against a hard immovable surface with gradually increasing force prior to his break. Takayuki Kubota even hits his hands and feet with hammers and weights, controlling the force and shock of his hammering until he's prepared for his materials.

PAIN: IS IT ALL IN THE MIND?

Although the martial arts has been a comparatively neglected field of interest as far as the medical profession is concerned, martial artists have incidentally benefited from research conducted in other areas of physical fitness and sport.

The fact is that there is a great deal of evidence amassed by experts over the years supporting a thesis that people who have experienced considerable pain have always considered somewhat obvious; namely, that pain is a relative experience that reflects not only damage or potential damage to the body, but also the mental attitude of the recipient or victim.

Randall "Tex" Cobb, a black belt in *Kojasho* karate, who came briefly into the public eye a few years ago when he survived a 15-round pounding given him by World Heavyweight Boxing Champion Larry Holmes, had already proved he could take a punch before he ever got into the ring with Holmes. He's survived not only a succession of heavyweight boxing matches but also a career that included a job bouncing drunks from some of the roughest bars in Albuquerque, New Mexico. I asked him once about the rumor that he'd been hit across the head with a tire iron and had stayed on his feet.

"Wasn't a tire iron," he said. "It was a crowbar." Though Cobb is a naturally funny man with a Texas fondness for stretched tales, those who saw him stay on his feet against Holmes will realize there's little reason for disbelieving him on this matter. In fact, during the course of our conversation he also said he'd been hit with a regulation Louisville Slugger baseball bat. "I been hit with everything, Sunshine, except a '54 Pontiac."

Interestingly enough, despite the baseball bat, the crowbar, and the fists of Larry Holmes, Cobb was the only boxer in a study done in conjunction with *Sports Illustrated* who was found to be without significant brain damage. That lack of brain damage, however, has nothing to do with his ability or lack of ability to experience pain. "Every time I get hit I get hurt," he asserted. "There is nothing whatever wrong with my nerve endings."

As a fighter, Cobb is accustomed to experiencing kicks and punches. Indeed, the expectation that he's going to be hit and kicked may, at least to some degree, transform the pain he experiences into something ranging from invigorating to bearable. In a series of articles writen on the subject of pain for *Karate Illustrated* magazine a number of years ago, Jim Mather cited the findings of a medical professional.

Quite a number of years ago, according to Mather, Dr. Henry Beecher, an anesthesiologist discovered that soldiers who had been wounded in battle were less inclined to require morphine for the pain they experienced than civilian patients who had recently `undergone surgery. Since Beecher was comparing battle wounds and surgery of a comparable nature, he was inclined to conclude that the experience of pain wasn't simply a matter of damaged bodies.

"There is no simple, direct relationship between the wound per se and the pain experienced," he reported. "The pain is in very large part determined by other factors, and of great importance here is the significance of the wound. In the wounded soldier the response to injury was relief, thankfulness at his escape alive from the battlefield, and even euphoria. To the civilian, his major surgery was a depressing, calamitous event."

Then there are the hair-raising tales of street punks high on PCP. High on this horse sedative, the user often becomes violent. This state of affairs is every cop's nightmare since the drug so totally blocks the experience of normal human pain that often it is all but impossible for several cops to subdue a small man.

Less violent and to some extent more remarkable to those of us raised in the Occident and conditioned to certain ideas about the importance of painkilling drugs are any number of videotaped major operations performed on wakeful patients in which acupuncture, implemented with a few needles, has been the only sedation required.

Doctors and nurses and coaches and athletes agree that the mind plays a big role in conveying or inhibiting the experience of pain. Just how big that role is has yet to be determined. To some degree, though, our attitude toward our pain is like a filter through which it must pass either to incapacitate us or to encourage us.

4
SAFETY AND INJURIES

Training in the martial arts provides any number of opportunities for acquiring injuries. In fact, it may be as dangerous as smoking cigarettes, eating improperly over a period of many years, climbing stairs, driving a car, or taking a shower in a slippery bathtub or shower stall. So be careful. Give up smoking, eat better, pay attention when climbing stairs, look where you're driving, and install rubber mats in the shower.

Likewise, in a martial arts context, warm up before stretching, stretch out before training, and tailor your training carefully to your *current* level of physical conditioning. If you're going to engage in breaking, at least condition your hands (or feet) to the shock of hitting solid objects and consider treating the skin beforehand with brine or some other skin-toughening solution to prevent tearing of the skin when striking. Beyond this brief discourse on the value of common sense, here are a few less obvious things you can do to enhance the safety of a break.

A SMALL CLOTH

One of the most common injuries experienced by breakers is a tearing, abrading, or lacerating of the knuckles against the rough surface of boards, bricks, and cinder blocks. Place a small cloth on top of the area you intend to strike—a record dust cloth is the perfect size and texture, though you can probably find something equally useful without incurring the expense. A piece of folded baby diaper or washcloth would probably provide equal protection. The cloth will not prevent your breakage, but it may spare you some splinters, injured knuckles, or bleeding.

PROTECTING YOUR ASSISTANTS

Remember in breaking that you also have to look out for the safety of your assistants. Before you take to the air to throw that jumping side kick through those boards, have a thought for your helpers. Make sure your breaking materials are large enough for them to grip solidly and still hold their hands out of the way of your strike. It's a good idea to have them place a towel or some sort of padding over their bare feet to protect them from chunks of wood or cinder block. Given the cost of oral surgery, it's also good to suggest that they be sure their mouths are closed at the moment of impact. They will anyway, but make sure you tell them that once they're properly braced and see you coming, they may close their eyes.

Your Audience

And now a word on behalf of the safety of the audience. It's not clear that your pet brown belt could or would ever bring suit against you for accidentally knocking his teeth out with a chunk of board. But in this day and age it's a fair guess that nearly any member of an audience would. If you're doing running jump kicks on the stage and you have an audience sitting six feet away and four feet below your helper, just where do you think those fragments of broken matter are going to end up?

Make it a rule not to set up a break until you have asked yourself if your assistants and the audience are safe from flying pieces of material. For you to do anything else would be negligent and potentially costly, both psychologically and monetarily.

INJURIES

In breaking, there are injuries and then there are injuries. Broken bones should be set by a doctor. Deep punctures of any sort should be seen and stitched by a doctor. Anytime you hit something (or are hit by something) and feel serious pain, experience nausea, or lose consciousness, you should seek immediate medical treatment.

Since you wouldn't be putting on a breaking display if you thought you were going to be hurt, it's unlikely that you will know the nearest source of medical treatment beforehand. The promoter of the event is likely to know, however, and in point of fact should probably have some competent medical assistance available at his event.

If it's only a relatively serious injury and not an absolute emergency, you may want to remember that many communities now have round-the-clock or nearly round-the-clock clinics. These are responsibly run medical care centers specializing in injuries requiring immediate attention. They have their own doctors and medical staffs and frequently advertise that they provide faster service than nearby hospital emergency rooms. Certainly they provide less expensive treatment.

Less serious injuries such as known strains or sprains, bruises, scratches, and minor cuts can be treated with ice and cold. Dr. Richard Birrer, a martial artist and an authority on martial arts injuries, cautions against soaking any puncture wound involving wood. Slivers of wood will swell with the water and become that much more difficult to remove.

Cold and Ice

Cold and ice are the miracle cures of modern sports medicine. Best of all, they are readily available from most faucets and refrigerators,

Tit Tah Jue is a Chinese medicinal liquid useful to Iron Palm students for both its healing and conditioning properties. Here, Richard Vera stands beside a vat of the pungent liquid. It is made, he explains, from 27 different herbs, minerals, and living things. It is said to stimulate the circulation of the blood, and Vera believes its regular use has prevented his hands from developing the calluses and calcification considered necessary by karate breakers.

are cheap, and are almost impossible to overdose on. They work especially well for simple swellings, cuts, bruises, and just general soreness. An added benefit is that the numbing quality of ice reduces pain.

Later on you may want to plan a trip to a nearby pharmacy. Drugstores and pharmacies sell any number of freezable bandages. Put them in your freezer until they've frozen and then wrap your sore limbs or joints. Often minor injuries can be wrapped and normal activities resumed.

Nonprescription Medicines
Favored by Martial Artists

Ed Brown, the breaker who loves pain, is a believer in brine.

"You get about 10 pounds of rock salt and put it in a five-gallon pail. Then," he says with a slight pause, "you put a medium-sized potato in it. When the potato finally comes to the top, you know you've got the Great Salt Lake in there, so you can start to soak. When the potato drops back down you know you've got to add some more salt. The idea is to heat up the water a little. You can soak your hands (and feet) for maybe 10 minutes a day. It helps heal up the little scratches and helps toughen them up at the same time. I myself don't soak much anymore, but I did when I was a beginner. The other thing it does is it helps protect your skin from a tendency to tear."

Tak Kubota sometimes rubs his hands and feet with vitamin E; Tit Tah Jue, of course, is the recommended salve of iron palm adept Richard Vera (see Chapter 9 for details). Runners and others swear by the value of DMSO, especially for joint injuries. For aches and pains, some kung fu schools with access to a Chinese community make use of a pungent brown ointment known as Tiger Balm. And then, of course, there are the good old American standbys: BandAids, Ben Gay, and aspirin.

5
KEYS TO SUCCESSFUL BREAKING

There are no gimmicks or tricks that can make you a successful breaker overnight. Mastery of this skill comes only after a great deal of practice, as well as the mental preparation discussed so far and the physical conditioning and training covered later in this book. You can, however, benefit from understanding a few factors that come into play in many endeavors and play a particularly important role in the martial arts and breaking.

RELAX TO FOCUS

In karate, the concept of *kime,* or focus, declares that a kick or punch should reach its maximum power and speed at the precise instant it makes contact with its target. A punch or kick that travels beyond that point in space is said to be *overextended.* By the same token, the technique that meets its target before achieving maximum force is said to be *jammed.*

In contrast to karate, the Chinese arts of kung fu seek what they often describe as *maximum penetration.* Less concerned with the visible and audible snap at the instant of impact, kung fu experts execute kicks and punches intended to

deliver their true damage potentials to sites deep within the body.

Luckily, whether we're talking about the concept of focus or *kime* in karate or the quality of penetration in kung fu, both arts claim that in part the ability to deliver power is derived from the skill of relaxation. For in its martial arts context, relaxation is just that: a skill that exists in relation to the absolute physical tension that follows and precedes it at the end of each technique.

In fact, since we can all execute the basic movements of the martial arts—lift so much weight, throw a ball, twist with a wrench, or push a stalled car—one might argue that relaxation is the main skill to be acquired by the martial artist. Knowing how and when to relax is a major aspect of any martial art or sport.

The concept of focus cannot be altogether foreign to anyone who has participated in or watched either golf or professional baseball. My earliest summer job involved caddying at a neighborhood country club. After I'd been at it awhile, I caddied in an occasional PGA tournament. I remember how much I marveled at the controlled relaxation of golf professional Julius

Boros. One of the game's all-time greats, and by then probably one of the oldest and most successful pros on tour, Boros had a swing that suggested that at the end of each club was a weight he could barely lift to the top of his backswing. And even as he started down toward the ball it was impossible to imagine he'd be able to hit the golf ball any farther than he could throw it. It was only in the last 70 degrees of his swing that his forearms bulged, face tightened into a grimace, and loose hips snapped down toward the ball. On impact, the club seemed suddenly too heavy again, resulting in a correct but extremely sluggish follow-through. Yet the result of this swing was inevitably a tee shot only 10 or 12 steps shorter than that of his younger rivals (and unfailingly much straighter). Boros, surely one of the great gentlemen of the game, knew how important relaxation and exertion were to the production of what golfers like to call *club head speed,* which is golf's equivalent of focus. (Does this explain the popularity of golf among martial artists?)

Steve Garvey, first baseman for the San Diego Padres, seems to have mastered the same sort of relaxation as a hitter, punching the ball from a very relaxed, upright stance, often hitting cannonball home runs out of the park with an effort that seems to have been reduced to a quick snapping motion of his massive forearms.

"Meditation," says Shihan Takayuki Kubota, "is very good for teaching the student how to relax. First of all, there is *ki,* which means 'focus.' Then there is meditation, which teaches relaxation. They go together because, if the student is not thinking about all kinds of other things, he's going to be relaxed. Then, when he's relaxed, he's going to be able to have the focus to make the break successfully. This means he will have confidence; he will break the materials in front of him."

Tae Kwon Do Master Hee Il Cho concurs. "If you are tense when you start to go into the break, it means you have some kind of doubt in your mind. Your concentration is not good, or maybe you're afraid of what's going to happen. So you're not going to make the break. You have to be completely relaxed."

KIAI

Kiai is another technique that promotes concentration. Thanks to the proliferation of martial arts movies, the *kiai,* or karate cry of attack, is an aspect of the martial arts at least superficially familiar to almost everyone.

On a physical level, the *kiai* is a shout or forcible expulsion of air intended to be voiced at the moment of a technique's maximum momentum and actual physical contact. Traditionally, the purpose of the *kiai* is to fill the opponent with a momentary, paralyzing fear and to assist the attacker in committing every remaining bit of physical and mental energy to the attack.

"The use of audible *kiai* is essential for learning the proper execution of techniques, for only then can the trainee 'fill' himself with enough concentration to trigger the release of his total spirit and therewith 'propel' his physical technique," writes Donn F. Draeger in his classic *Modern Bujutsu and Budo.*

The *kiai* ought not to be thought of as a mere shout of attack, however. For one thing, traditional martial artists insist that the cry originates not in the vocal cords and lungs, but from the stomach, or from what the Japanese like to call the *hara* (located in the body's center of gravity, approximately three inches below the navel).

Many traditional karate *kata,* or forms, practices call for the martial artist to *kiai* on the execution of various techniques. Otherwise, in many respects the traditional *kiai* has never been particularly fashionable in America. In spurning "unscientific" martial arts traditions having to do with the development of *ki* or the *kiai,* contemporary *karateka* and kung fu adepts seem to have made every effort to adopt and perfect only the most physical elements, as though martial arts training were a purely physical exercise that might be extracted from a swamp of irrelevant sentiment and hocus-pocus.

Nevertheless, it is my observation that the *kiai* is used widely among martial arts experts who have developed breaking skills. Many martial artists who otherwise take no interest in Zen or meditation or yoga do not hesitate at all to emit a blood-curdling *kiai* before breaking through a stack of boards or bricks. Likewise, the value of such an expulsion of breath or, if you will, war cry, is one of the few things on which it would seem karate and kung fu agree. Even Bruce Lee, at least early in his career, believed in both breaking and *kiai.*

In fact, probably nobody did more to make the *kiai* famous to the movie-going public than the late Bruce Lee. In fighting scenes from the 3½ films that did so much to bring him fame in the late '60s and early '70s, Lee's *kiai* sounds hawklike, positively unearthly, and not at all like the exhaling shout of a karate practitioner. This, as he would claim later, was pure histrionics.

In fact, in a rare book purportedly written by Lee some 10 years before his death and later republished by Latino H. Gonzales as *Bruce Lee's Modern Gung Fu Karate* in the Philippines (where lack of international copyright agreements makes such things possible), the text has Lee recommending that the student voice the sound *sot,* a word said to mean "kill" or "execute" in Chinese.

Though Lee would later renounce many of his previously expressed and published ideas, this early work contains quite a lot of information of value to martial artists wanting to prepare themselves for the trials of breaking. Perhaps Lee's wife, Linda, will one day consider having it properly republished (and protected by American copyright laws).

With respect to the use of the word *sot,* Lee goes on to tell the reader that, like the *kiai* of karate, it must be employed at the moment of maximum exertion in any breaking situation. The cry recommended by Lee originates from the same abdominal area as the *kiai (tanden* to the Japanese; Chinese stylists usually name it *don tien* or *tanten).* Lee takes it a step further, as well. According to his view, as expressed in about 1963, Lee believed that during weight training or resistance exercises martial artists should establish the habit of always exhaling from this area at the moment of maximum physical exertion while lifting the weights during a bench press, for instance, or lifting the body in a push-up. Echoing traditional Chinese kung fu teaching, Lee explains without the later skepticism he would become known for that kung fu is more dependent on "breath strength" than on "body strength."

THE *HARA*

According to most historical Asian thought and teaching, the center of balance and perhaps the physical soul exists somewhere between the navel and the groin. For the martial artist this point represents a center of both balance and physical power. It is called by many names, from

ABDOMINAL CRUNCH: Among the many reasons that strong abdominal muscles are important is that they enable you to keep your hips properly tucked or rotated forward and underneath your upper body. By keeping your legs elevated as in these photos, you'll protect your lower back from the lower back strain often caused by sit-ups and place all the stress on your abdominals.

chakra to *hara* to *tanden,* and is almost always considered the source of the life force *ki* or *chi* or whatever else you might care to call it.

Many martial arts systems teach deep breathing exercises in an effort to awaken the student's awareness of the importance of this area as a source of both spiritual power and physical energy. Yet even those who avoid this subtle aspect of training—almost all of them—teach something intended to make the student conscious of the vast physical power that can be generated when this area of the body is properly harnessed through good martial arts technique.

Hirokazu Kanazawa, one of the first men to complete the Japanese Karate Association instructor's course in 1956, is a man very widely respected in knowledgeable martial arts circles. Martial artists who've trained rigorously for 20 years and more will become positively dewy-eyed in talking about his historic karate matches in the '50s. In fact, many knowledgeable black belts quite plainly insist that he has the best technique they have ever seen.

Proper breathing from the *hara,* Kanazawa insists, is extremely important to the execution of good martial arts technique. To help students learn the importance of exhaling at the proper instant, Kanazawa teaches a drill in which the breath is expelled from the *hara* at the instant the karate punch achieves maximum focus and theoretical impact. In the drill the assistant places his hand on the lower abdomen of a partner, applying a sharp slap at the instant the partner's punch reaches maximum momentum. This drill, according to Kanazawa, imparts a very precise knowledge of when to exhale and assists the martial artist in developing maximum power for the punch.

6
PHYSICAL CONDITIONING

Several years ago, a nonrunning friend of mine was inspired to take up running on the basis of watching Alberto Salazar's world record marathon race. With the help of his pocket calculator, he broke down Salazar's total time and found the Oregon runner ran all 26.2 miles at a pace of just a little over five minutes per mile. The friend therefore figured that a six-minute mile (especially since he was going to run only one) was a realistic time in which to run the mile circuit from his house to a neighborhood park and home again. He didn't discuss his plan with anyone and, since he'd been playing tennis for many years, figured he was in relatively decent physical condition. So he went down to a nearby sporting goods store, bought a pair of shoes recommended by a popular running magazine, did a couple of perfunctory stretches he'd seen other runners do, and suffered a severe hamstring tear about halfway through his first mile (since high school 10 years before).

He was trying to make up for lost time, he explained later, even deceiving himself into thinking he might be able to run the last half-mile in 2 minutes (having required 4 to run the first half). It was about 15 months later, still inspired by Salazar, that my friend finally ran his first mile. His time, by the way, was 7 minutes and 14 seconds. By then, of course, he'd taken the trouble to educate himself somewhat. He learned that those 5½-minute recovery miles of Salazar's were many hard years in the making. Finally, my friend was willing to take a realistic view of the vast gulf that separated his early ambition from the achievement of one of the best marathoners ever. By then, he was quite proud of himself for being able to run a single mile in 6½ minutes.

This same mix of haste, ambition, and foolhardiness is equally common—perhaps more so—in the martial arts. I remember very vividly the first breaking demonstration I ever saw. One of the breakers was newly arrived in the highly competitive martial arts community of Los Angeles, and after making a great to-do about the empty beer bottle he was carrying up on stage, stood up under the bright lights, and bashed the bottle across the crown of his head. The bottle broke, all right. A pleased expression appeared on his face—and then, abruptly, a look of doubt. Freeing one of his hands from the neck of the broken bottle, he touched his head and brought his hand down covered with blood, blood that was brightly illuminated by the spotlight that beamed down on him. He ran from the hall (presumably in the direction of one of the many hospitals nearby).

Several years ago, a black belt with whom I'd struck up an acquaintance suggested that, if I really wanted to understand something about the martial arts, I should begin to read translations of some of the Asian writings on the arts of war and strategy. Highly recommended was the classic of sword strategy, Miyamoto Musashi's *A Book of Five Rings.* In fact, I'd been reading it one evening before going out to a full-contact karate program that was to be written up for a karate magazine that employed me as an editor.

Miyamoto Musashi is to traditional Japan something between a god and a hero. Indeed, this master swordsman of 17th century Japan is widely regarded as perhaps the greatest individual warrior who ever lived, especially by martial artists.

Having chosen the historically "wrong" side in the battle of Seki ga Hara in siding with the Hideyoshi faction instead of the ultimately victorious Tokugawa Ieyasu, the man who was to become the first Tokugawa shogun, or military dictator, of Japan, Musashi became a renegade, or *ronin,* samurai—a warrior without a retainer or lord—a "swordslinger" devoted to perfecting his sword art for its own sake. Over time, Musashi became the ultimate swordsman, the consummate samurai, who defeated more than 60 challengers.

Perhaps the thing that impressed me most about Musashi was the fact that, as time went on, he seemed to disdain the use of a sword and instead killed his opponents with wooden practice swords, carved oars, and freshly cut sticks. He'd become so skilled that he often slept on beaches and killed with green branches the enemies who came to meet him with what must have been the most beautiful and carefully crafted swords in Japan. His training and preparation were such that, against the most refined killing weapons of his day, Musashi needed only a stick to defeat and kill his enemies.

With the tales of Musashi fresh in my mind, I went out to the full-contact karate debut of a black belt with a reputation as an outstanding tournament competitor and, unfortunately, an

excellent street fighter. We'll call him Joe. To all outward intents and appearances he was prepared. That is to say, his hair had been styled, his stylish *gi* bottoms had been carefully contoured around his muscled legs, and his upper body glistened with definition. From his animated state of mind and excitement level before the bout, most people in the audience probably believed they were watching the eventual winner of the match. By contrast, his opponent (we'll call him Jim) was a bit on the pale side; his *gi* bottoms were nothing special, and he seemed rather more frightened than excited, especially when Joe came out to the center of the ring to listen to the referee's instructions before the match. Joe stared at Jim with pure malevolence. And Jim didn't seem to want even to glance at Joe.

What a one-minute burst of effort in the ring! Joe dashed out after Jim and threw every jump-spin-kick combination he'd ever dreamed up. He threw straight punches, uppercuts, backfists, ridge hands, jabs, and hooks, one after another. Jim kept his hands over his head, constantly busy just trying to stay out of the way. Joe managed to keep this onslaught up for the better part of two rounds. By the beginning of the third round, though, it was obvious that he was tired. Now Jim began to throw an occasional counter, and Joe began to develop trouble moving out of the way. As the round progressed, Joe got hit more and more often—not with flashy techniques, but with compact, short punches, mostly to the body. As the round was entering the last seconds, Joe panicked and tried to run away. His corner was angry with him and kept yelling for him not to turn his back on his opponent. Meanwhile Jim kept coming steadily forward, holding his hands high, closing the gap with front snap kicks, and following up with straight lefts. Joe was doing very little of anything now except trying to run away. Finally, Joe draped himself over the ropes and let his tired arms hang down toward the audience. The bell rang, signaling that Jim had won the fight on the basis of what was too mercifully ruled a TKO. The audience was filled with people who knew Joe by his tournament skills and his reputation as one tough hombre. It must have been a bitter lesson. In fact, I don't think I ever saw Joe again.

Joe was simply not prepared for the demands

of full-contact karate. Luckily, he was not injured—at least not physically—in incurring his first and probably only loss. You, as an aspiring breaker, cannot hope for Joe's luck. You will probably be injured if you attempt to learn how to break without first putting yourself through some fairly rigorous preparation.

POWER AND THE HIPS

Over the centuries, the martial arts have developed a remarkable number of striking surfaces—hands, elbows, fingertips, knees, feet, forearms, head, and thighs, to name only a few. These techniques travel from every conceivable angle to a multitude of targets. Yet the one thing these striking surfaces all share is the fact that each ultimately draws its power from the hips or pelvic area.

Masatoshi Nakayama, chief instructor for the largest traditional karate organization in the world, the Japanese Karate Association, regards the hips as vital to the production of martial arts power. Indeed, he compares the hips with a spring, suggesting that the more tightly the hips are cocked, the greater the power they will unleash in the technique when it arrives at its target. In this he is far from alone.

In fact, basic martial arts stances, in both kung fu and karate, all require properly tucked hips—that is, pelvis held in a rolled-forward position directly under the ribs, with the abdominal muscles tightened. In fact, if you're training regularly, probably nearly half the calisthenics, stretches, and exercises you do are intended to increase your awareness of this vital area.

The following exercises and other drills appearing in the remainder of the book make no claim to being either exhaustive or definitive. They are included here entirely as a supplement to your regularly scheduled workouts. Actually, the few routines appearing herein have been selected because they seem to pinpoint areas of special interest to those who want to prepare themselves for the special demands of breaking. In addition to these, there exists a wealth of other exercises and drills. Finding and stressing areas of potential weakness, since weaknesses are an individual matter, is a task left to the student.

HIP CIRCLES: This exercise is valuable for increasing the strength of hip and abdominal areas. Lie flat on your back with your arms spread out while bending your knees. While keeping your lower back flat on the floor, turn your legs to the right and left. A useful variation can be done with the legs straight. Photos continue on pages 26–27.

Hip Circles continued.

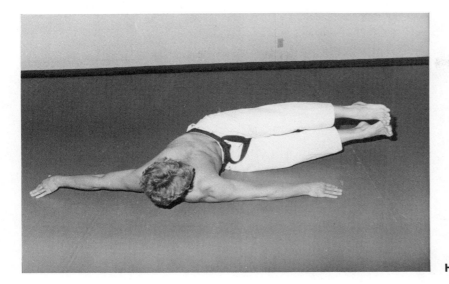

Hip Circles concluded.

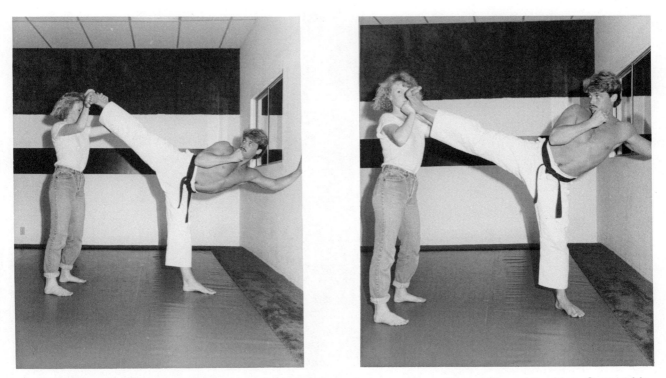

SIDE STRETCH (HIP PLACEMENT): Powerful kicks depend very much on the position of the hips. Correct hip position ensures that all the body's muscles are involved in the kick. In this exercise support yourself against a wall or post and have your partner raise your kicking leg out and up, lifting the leg slowly higher as you can feel the muscles stretch. When doing this partner-assisted side kick stretch, it is essential to keep the hips aligned with the supporting leg and not to allow them to rotate to either side.

FRONT KICK STRETCH (HIP PLACEMENT):
Note in the first photo that the model loses power in allowing his right hip to rise. In contrast, by keeping his hips level and his upper body more upright, as in the second photo, he is able to deliver substantially more power to his target.

INCREASING STRENGTH

Some rather special physical demands are placed on the person who wants to learn to break. To hit something hard enough to break it is to subject various parts of your body to unaccustomed levels of physical shock. A mere toughening of the hands, feet, or elbows, while it may make them tough enough to withstand the counterforce of striking hard surfaces, will not do much to prepare you to absorb the shock to supporting muscles and joints.

Shihan Tak Kubota made this point over coffee in a Los Angeles area restaurant. He mimed throwing a standard reverse punch and then, with a hand swollen by 30 years of calluses and broken bones, pointed to critical stress areas. "If you want to break," he said, "you must be strong at the hip, the shoulder, the elbow, the wrist, and then finally at the knuckles. It's the same with the kick. Toes, ankles, knees must be ready."

While there is no end to the exercises suitable for strengthening or lengthening muscle groups for the martial arts, the intention here is to include only a few of those that specifically address areas already discussed in the text.

Some of the following exercises, such as knuckle push-ups, have been chosen because they do double duty, conditioning striking surfaces while increasing strength, or stretching muscles while also strengthening them, and so on. Yet other exercises have been selected for the clarity with which they isolate a given muscle group: the idea behind this is to focus sharply on the muscles in question and encourage the student to concentrate on exercises that work troublesome areas.

These exercises and drills do not pretend to be a complete workout and are meant only to supplement your training. Most fitness experts now recommend a training schedule of every other day. This every-other-day regimen should be something you work up to, though. The beginner would be ill-advised to attempt to condition his hands and feet with such regularity at first. Don't attempt to harden striking surfaces when they're still in pain from an earlier session. Wait until all but minor discomfort has subsided and then begin again—slowly.

POWER KICKING DRILL: A partner with a heavy pad can provide mobility or stability and prepare the breaker for both the shock of resistance and kicking something held by a human assistant. In this sequence, the model steps into a powerful side kick that drives his assistant toward the wall.

DEVELOPING HAND AND FOREARM STRENGTH:
Grippers such as the one pictured above are
available in varying degrees of difficulty at most
athletic stores. They can be carried in the car and
used in traffic jams. A number of squeezable
puttylike grip-strengthening products (below and
right) are also generally available. By bracing your
forearm against your knee before squeezing, you'll
prevent yourself from "cheating" or using muscles
other than those in the forearm. Hold your fist
vertical or horizontal and, since the thumb serves as
a latch to keep your fist locked, use your thumb as
well.

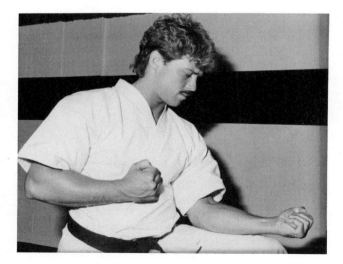

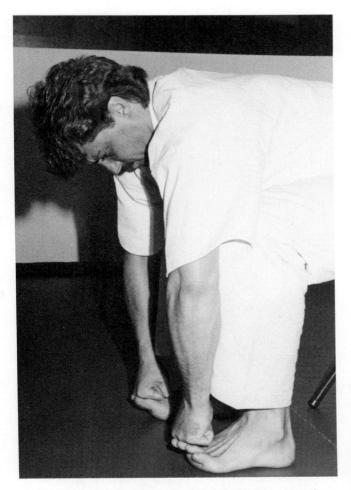

TOE-STRENGTHENING EXERCISES: Strong and flexible toes are essential for developing balance and solid stances. Exercised toes are easier to control as well. You can strengthen your toes by providing the resistance of your fists. Put your fists down over your toes and then, using only the muscles in your feet, try to lift your toes against the pressure of your fists. Place a towel or other cloth on the floor and then, from a sitting position, pull it toward you with curling and uncurling motions of your toes.

**KUNG FU IRON PALM CONDITIONING—
CHOPSTICKS:** As shown here, kung fu master
Richard Vera rolls bundled and tied chopsticks
between the palms of his hands. He is breathing
here from the *tanten* and radiating his strength into
his hands. By holding his hands upright (in a
prayer-like position), he uses different muscles than
he uses in the accompanying photo where the
twisting motion used is similar to that used in trying
to remove a cap from the neck of a bottle or tube. In
both maneuvers he continues to apply the same
breathing and concentration principles.

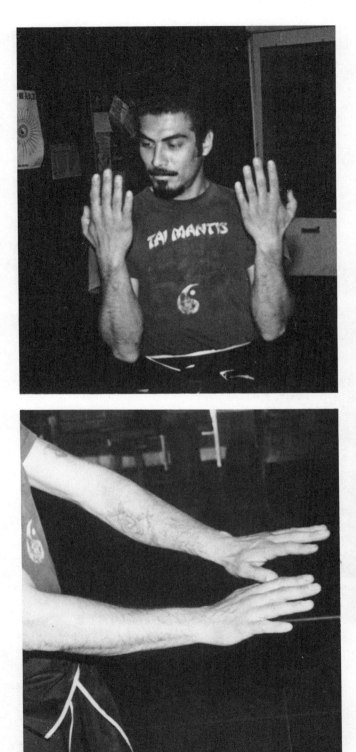

HEAVY HANDS: In kung fu the most desirable quality in a martial arts kick or punch is considered to be penetration. In these three views of Richard Vera's hands, while it is not possible to see their ability to penetrate, their size, muscularity, and lack of calcification are certainly apparent.

PARTNER-ASSISTED RESISTANCE EXERCISES:
Even the most expensive training equipment in the
world can't provide the encouragement of a training
partner. In these exercises, a training partner uses
her arms and body weight to provide resistance to
the model's vital leg motions. In the first two photos
the model first pushes the leg upward against
resistance and then, to work the opposing muscle
group, pulls downward as in the next two photos.
This drill will develop strength for the front,
roundhouse, and hook kicks. In the final drill side
kick, strength is developed along the same principle.

The Push-Up

Say the word *exercise* or *calisthenics* and most
probably your listener is going to have a vision
of somebody doing a push-up. While it's hard to

say something new about an exercise most people have been taking for granted for years, it's
possible to derive more specific martial arts
benefits by improving the quality of those push-
ups you're already doing. Letting the punching
arm pull the shoulder too far forward diminishes
the power of the punch. The student is often
enjoined to keep the shoulder down in punching
to prevent the shoulder from moving forward
from the chest. In the ideal push-up, as in the
ideal training punch, the shoulders are inte-
grated with the rest of the upper body, and the
shoulder blades tend to occupy a lower position
in the back. Therefore, when doing push-ups,
concentrate on keeping the scapula bones down
(toward the waistline) and the shoulders per-

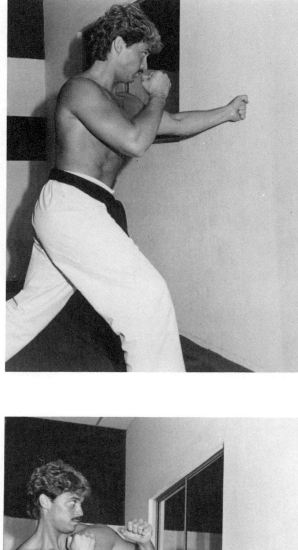

WALL RESISTANCE TRAINING: When no partner is available, similar benefits may be had by using the natural resistance provided by a solid wall. The idea here is to position the limb as though you are actually kicking or hitting the wall. Now exert the same muscles you would use in kicking a human target. This drill is useful in correcting minor weaknesses in balance and alignment. Improper wrist alignment during the punch, for example, will cause the wrist to buckle in the direction of its weakness.

fectly squared in front. For maximum benefit, do fewer push-ups much more slowly. Feel those areas where you are weak and force yourself to travel more slowly through those ranges of comparative weakness.

Knuckle Push-Ups

These are intended to develop strength while conditioning the knuckles. Start out on softer surfaces first and then work your way toward harder—cement probably being the ultimate surface here. Remember that in punching you'll be breaking primarily with the first two knuckles, so concentrate the stress of the push-ups against these two knuckles.

Fingertip Push-Ups

These push-ups are intended to strengthen your fingers and hands. In doing them, you will notice that there is considerable difference between the stress placed on hands that are only slightly curled and the discomfort experienced when you are really high up on the tips of your fingers. Experiment with different elevations. Force your-

self to move slowly, concentrating on good form and keeping your shoulder blades down.

Back-of-the-Hand Push-Ups

These may come slowly at first. However, since the wrists are truly the most highly stressed joints in a punch, strengthening them, especially for breaking, is essential. As these push-ups become easier, you may move to harder surfaces and derive the double benefit of strengthening the wrists and conditioning the backs of the hands. Remember, it's better to do a few using good form than many with sloppy technique.

PUSH-UPS: Especially if done on hard, rough surfaces, push-ups can be useful in developing conditioned skin and increasing strength. The idea here is to put the stress where you want it. Illustrated here and on page 38 are push-ups done on the knuckles, fingertips, backs of the hands, and thumbs. In developing the muscles used in the punch, push-ups are most useful when they are done with the hands at about shoulder level, while making an effort to use more than just your upper shoulder muscles.

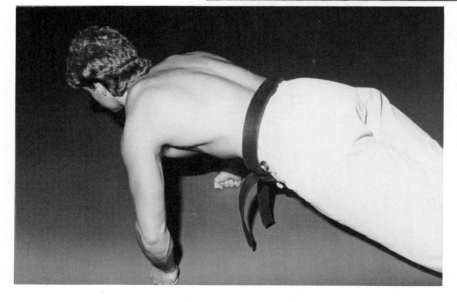

PUSH-UPS: Concentrate on preventing the shoulder blades from rising toward your shoulders and keeping them pushed down toward your hips, as in the last photo in this series.

7
TRAINING AND WARMING UP

With the advent of full-contact karate in the early '70s, the martial arts world was obliged to take a closer look at the boxing world it had largely scorned. It was an embarrassing time in the history of American martial arts. Most karate black belts and advanced kung fu students were at least partly convinced that they had developed the much-heralded power of their Asian masters. Indeed, one of the most prevalent anxieties of the early full-contact fighters centered around the possibility that one of the punches or kicks they'd been practicing for many years might prove fatal to an opponent or, worse, that the receipt of such a kick or punch might bring about their own deaths.

Hitosuki hitogeri, a Japanese phrase meaning "one kick, one punch," asserted for the traditional martial artist the only true and ideal essence of karate. Simply, the trained martial artist ought to put an end to any self-defense encounter with this absolute economy of technique. This phrase, commonly attributed to Mas Oyama, expresses a radical karate ideal from which most modern martial arts practitioners have strayed a good deal.

During the early '70s, while some martial arts traditionalists persisted in the belief that their kicks and punches were indeed at least potentially deadly, other, notably younger, martial artists began to question such an assumption—actually, challenge it is more accurate.

A young Hong Kong-born kung fu fanatic and teacher named Bruce Lee was one of the principal rebels. He broke with cultural taboos against teaching kung fu to non-Chinese, questioned the theoretical assertions of kung fu classicists, studied boxing, and generally demanded proof of the effectiveness of a martial arts technique before he would add it to his personal repertoire.

Among martial artists, however, another renegade had a similar if not greater impact. Joe Lewis, the man who would become the original American karate superstar, had returned home from a stint in the Marines even cockier than he'd been when he departed. He was a skilled and intimidating fighter, almost impossible to beat. He seemed to be unafraid of man or beast and defeated nearly all his opponents. Unlike, say, the modest and sincere Chuck Norris, Lewis did not hesitate to criticize and guffaw. And unlike Lee, who often seemed to prefer to demonstrate his prowess on people outside the arts, Lewis did not hesitate to spar with and defeat any and all comers. That willingness to back up his own arrogance and outspokeness made him a natural hero to a generation of modern American martial artists who wanted a martial arts training that would serve them outside the genteel atmosphere of the *dojo,* or karate school.

In the late '60s, the outspoken Lewis stepped outside his karate origins and began to train with Bruce Lee and boxer Joey Orbillo. Lewis, who had won karate tournament grand championship after grand championship, now seemed shamelessly to seek something not found in karate dogma or in what seemed to him a blind belief in martial arts traditions. In 1970 Lewis is said to have fought the first American full-contact karate bout, knocking out Greg Baines in the second round at the Long Beach Arena. When Baines and Lewis both survived, many discontented martial artists suddenly developed an interest in boxing and in the learning potentials of actual physical contact.

THE HEAVY BAG

No long after Lewis began to dabble in boxing, traditional karate instructors were often shocked and even angry to find their students carrying around boxing magazines. And in *dojo* after *dojo,* the heavy bag began to swing from the rafters.

The heavy bag is a useful adjunct to the traditional Japanese *makiwara* board (discussed later in this chapter), and, of course, to the speed bag. Although the rough surface of the heavy bag will, over time, condition the knuckles, its primary purpose is to accustom the martial artist to the kind of resistance experienced when hitting something both heavy and absorbent. The type of resistance offered by the heavy bag provides the martial artist with an opportunity both to experience what it's like to hit something heavy and to put at risk the joints that will be stressed on contact.

Training on the heavy bag is particularly desirable for those who want to become adept at breaking, since the potentially fortifying shock experienced by the joints involved in breaking is so similar to that produced by strikes against the heavy bag.

Happily, punching the heavy bag with moderate to full force can correct your technique, usually more gently than any actual breaking. In punching, you will feel the bag's shock waves travel through your hand to your wrist and elbow and then up into your shoulders and finally down into your hips and legs. Likewise, in kicking, the shock will pass through your ankles, knees, hips, and into your upper body. If your wrist is not aligned properly, you will strain or sprain it. If your elbow is not positioned properly, you will likewise experience a warning in that joint. Hence, as you learn to strike the heavy bag with increasing effectiveness, you are also learning to correct your own form. It won't do to try to punch either a brick or a human being with a limp wrist, and the heavy bag is a fairly patient teacher of such truths.

It is advisable for a variety of reasons to separate the training done on the heavy bag from the hand and foot conditioning you may be doing on the *makiwara* board or against other surfaces. Since to derive maximum benefit from your heavy bag you will want to work in the direction of going all out, eventually kicking and punching with an absolute maximum of effort, it is advisable to tape and glove the hands.

The hands should be taped in such a way as to cover the first knuckles and the back of the wrist. The tape should be wrapped around the hand and forearms without restricting circulation. When you make a fist you should feel considerable tension in the wrist and forearm areas, and the knuckles should be at least partly protected from the abrading power of the bag. Even after your hands are sufficiently conditioned, you should retain the tape along the backs of your hands to prevent injuring the relatively delicate bones there. You can go all out on the heavy bag much sooner than you can go all out on the *makiwara* board. Thus, on the heavy bag you'll be conditioning joints and muscle groups. On the *makiwara* you'll be conditioning actual striking surfaces.

MAKIWARA TRAINING

There is possibly no more enlightening story about the effectiveness of *makiwara* board training than the one karate writer Dave Lowry tells of Gigo Funakoshi. The son of Gichin Funako-

Text continues on page 44.

THE HEAVY BAG—PUNCHING: The heavy bag is useful in that it provides stress for the joints that will be stressed by breaking, minor conditioning of the striking surfaces, and also occasionally uncomfortable correction of technique. Common punching errors that will get the breaker in trouble include wrists improperly aligned upward or downward as in the first two photos (left and below left), as well as a "wandering" thumb, shown in the third photo. Proper punching, as in the two photos on top of page 42, requires strong wrists aligned properly. Note, too, that contact is made with the heavy bag just before the punch is fully extended.

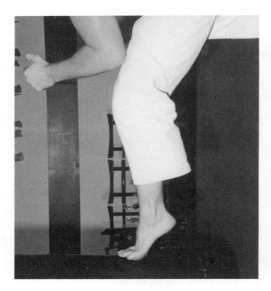

THE HEAVY BAG—KICKING: Toes represent one of the major hazards of kicking the heavy bag. Though Shihan Tak Kubota prefers to break boards with his big toe on some kicks, this is emphatically not advisable for the untrained beginner and would result in a certain broken toe at least for the unprepared. The first kick shows toes improperly curled back. The second kick shows toes properly pulled back. Only after you've become very successful at keeping your toes curled back should you feel ready to blast away.

ELBOW ALIGNMENT AND FOREARM ROTATION: In an abbreviated version of the traditional punch, the model illustrates the importance of keeping the elbow close to the body as the punch starts and proceeds toward its target. Note as well the slow rotation of the forearm in which the punch is not fully turned over even in the fourth photo, but is still twisting up until the moment of impact.

shi, the man most people consider modern Japanese karate's founding father, the younger Funakoshi reportedly attributed his powerful punches to the many hours he spent pounding on the *makiwara* board. On several occasions the younger Funakoshi inadvertently performed the not-at-all-simple task of actually breaking the *makiwara* board with his powerful practice punches.

What is the *makiwara* board? Traditionally, it is a redwood two-by-four board about seven feet long, stuck in the ground or bolted to the floor and used as a target for various karate punches and strikes. Rope is typically wound about the board at punching height. The rope is often covered with a basketball knee pad or strips of canvas or sometimes wrapped with tape. Thus the martial artist has a rough (but not too rough), strong, and relatively unyielding surface against which to condition his striking surfaces.

Makiwara is Japanese for "padded board," and as a training device it has been in use in Okinawa for centuries. Though it is often neglected as a training tool in the United States, the *makiwara* board is extremely useful to those who want to condition and harden their limbs to the shock of hard contact.

Outdoor *makiwara* are easily made from seven-foot lengths of redwood. About two feet of the board are buried in the earth, and the topmost three feet are gradually beveled to about an inch in thickness. Traditional indoor versions that bolt to the floor can be purchased from martial arts supply houses. These are similar in every way to the outdoor types, though board length is shorter since these are usually bolted to the floor. Mounting, seating, and proper bevel are vital to the *makiwara,* since these factors determine the all-important give of the board when it is struck. What you're looking for is a little like a diving board in resistance. For just as appropriate board resistance enables a champion Olympic diver like Greg Louganis to experience something very close to perfect form and unassisted human flight, so a similar resistance in a *makiwara* enables the martial artist to develop his own form and timing, as well as speed, power, and the desired conditioning of the striking and blocking parts of the body.

The *makiwara* board is easily homemade, though for most people it is probably as easily acquired through one of the many martial arts supply houses that advertise in the martial arts magazines or in the Yellow Pages.

In addition to the traditional boards, there are numerous other products on the market that may come to serve nearly as effectively as the traditional *makiwara* boards. A quick perusal of the ads in any of the major martial arts magazines will reveal a surprisingly wide variety of substitutes.

There are durable and resistant pads that can be fastened to the wall for around $10, and there are any number of products with rough surfaces and resistant properties that, intelligently used, may well be as effective as the *makiwara.*

To Shihan Tak Kubota there is not much purpose to blocking unless you can hope to hurt your opponent with your block. That's why he believes in the *makiwara.*

As with virutally every training apparatus you have access to, your workout on the *makiwara* should be regular and of gradually increasing difficulty. Unless your hands have already been toughened through training or because of the work you do, the tenderness of your knuckles and the ease with which your skin is torn will require you to set a very moderate pace for your *makiwara* training.

In fact, before you begin pounding on the board with your fists, you would be well advised to prepare yourself on the heavy bag and other relatively padded surfaces. It is essential that your wrists, elbow joints, and shoulders be up to the rigors of the board. Dave Lowry and Ed Brown recommend that students with delicate skin condition their hands in salt water in order to prevent scrapes and tears.

Moderation will take you farther faster. Rather than succumbing to the temptation to push yourself the way you might on a long run, it is better to start out with a few strikes per session and add incrementally to your total as you find that your striking surfaces are free of pain.

Once you've begun to improve your standard punching technique you can add other strikes. Ridge hands, backfists, palm strikes, elbows, and forearms can be added in the same gradual increments.

Part of the beauty of the traditional *makiwara* consists of the "feel" it imparts on recoil. Over time you will learn to read it and improve your technique based on the feedback given by the post as it snaps back in response to your blow. In this respect, *makiwara* substitutes attached to walls and doors are both more potentially dangerous and less responsive. These latter can offer you precious little by way of an evaluation of your speed and focus.

Lowry warns that too zealous a use of the *makiwara* by the beginner can result in a need for surgery. It is necessary to toughen the skin, he observes, before you begin to acquire scar tissue around the joints of your fingers. There is also, Lowry asserts, some body of medical opinion that believes that repeated punching of the *makiwara* or breaking may lead to arthritis and other diseases of the joints. Those who suffer from arthritis or gout or who have a history of those diseases in their immediate families will probably want to consult their physicians before attempting to put such stress on their joints.

ON WARMING UP
Speaking specifically of tournament karate and what he supposes is a lack of recognition from

Text continues on page 49.

MAKIWARA CONDITIONING FOR HANDS, ELBOWS, AND FOREARMS: As shown here by Shihan Takayuki Kubota, the *makiwara* board lends itself to a wide variety of strikes. Some of the strikes regularly employed by Kubota include, in the order shown above and on pages 46–47, the straight punch, knuckle punch, outside hooking elbow strike, inside hooking elbow strike, inside elbow thrust, knifehand strike, backfist strike, inverted knifehand strike, palm heel strike, and hammerfist strike.

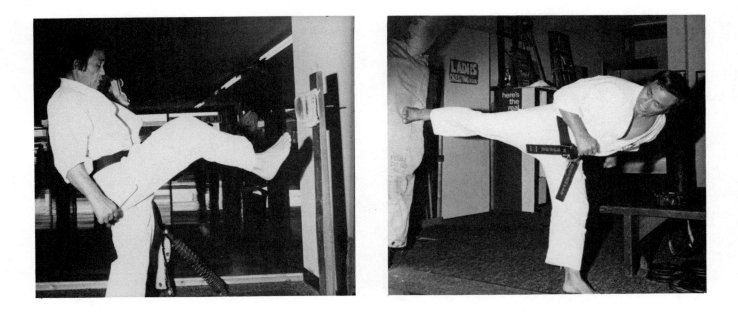

CONDITIONING THE FEET, TOES, AND SHINS ON THE *MAKIWARA* **AND OTHER SURFACES:** Tak Kubota conditions feet and legs on both the traditional *makiwara* and a homemade device made by one of his students. There are any number of useful products or innovations useful in karate conditioning. The *makiwara* with the car tire is a device used by the baseball bat–breaking Shihan Joko Ninomiya.

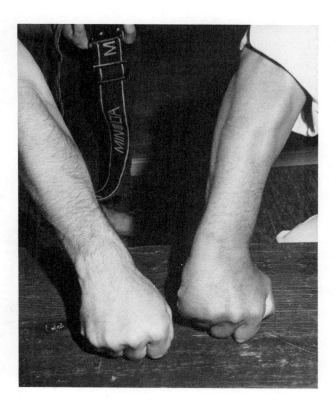

HANDS CONDITIONED AND UNCONDITIONED:
As shown here on the right-hand side of each photo, Shihan Tak Kubota compares his hand and fist, conditioned by 46 years of karate, with the hand and fist of a non-martial artist.

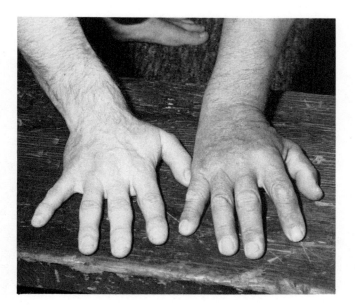

the champions of earlier times, national point fighting champion Steve "Nasty" Anderson told a magazine interviewer not long back, "All the other sports except this one have admitted to the fact that the [new] guys are better." Because of Anderson's unpopular and not particularly aesthetic fighting style, this remark undoubtedly raised some hackles in the karate community.

In at least one sense, though, Anderson is perfectly correct. Unless statistics lie, athletes do get better. Year in, year out, local, regional, national, and international records in all sports continue to improve. It's a matter of record that the athlete of today is taller, stronger, more muscular, and remains active longer than earlier generations would have thought possible.

Chief among the reasons for this, of course, are breakthroughs in nutrition and medicine that enable us to live longer and healthier lives. Also significant, though, is the fact that athletic training has become very specific. Computerized training centers such as the Coto de Caza Research Center in Orange County in California can take high-speed films of athletes in action and then enhance athletic performance by providing the athletes with sometimes small and

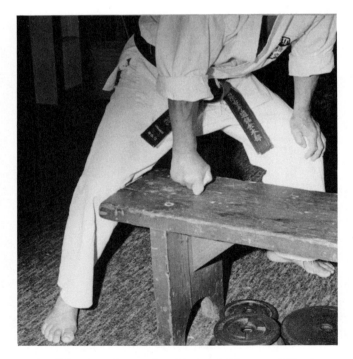

Anything wooden or hard is useful for conditioning striking surfaces. In these two photos, applying principles of compression, Kubota toughens the knuckle of an index finger and the backs of his hands.

extremely localized exercises intended to improve athletic performance over a very short range of movement. Weight training machines can be programmed to work these very small ranges of certain muscle groups, producing in a short time very large total efficiency gains for the athlete.

Career longevity is another factor that goes into producing contemporary athletic excellence. It only stands to reason that an athlete who suffers no appreciable physical deterioration is going to get better and better in his or her particular event with each opportunity to practice or compete. From distance runners to baseball pitchers, athletes are staying healthy and active for longer periods of time. And while it would be a mistake not to credit modern sports medicine with having brought about some of these gains, surely athletes and their coaches deserve some credit for their interest in maintaining very high levels of physical fitness.

One of the most modern and revolutionary ideas in athletic circles is that any athletic endeavor ought to be preceded by both warming up and stretching out.

The Warm-Up

Though each sport has its own requirements, and though you will probably want to warm up different muscle groups more thoroughly for sparring, a medium to light warm-up is definitely called for prior to breaking.

According to modern sports medicine authorities, even moderate stretching should be preceded by a warm-up period. It is a well established physiological fact that anything the human body can do at a normal temperature it can do slightly better at a warmer one. In part, the idea here is simply to elevate the heart and breathing rate, to get the body to produce a physical sensation of warmth and a corresponding rise in heart rate and blood temperature. Running in place, shadowboxing, jumping rope, doing a few sit-ups and push-ups rapidly, punching a light bag—combinations of these done for a few minutes before your breaking will make you capable of faster and stronger muscular contractions and thus provide you with a power edge. Remember, perspiration is usually the most reliable indicator that you are in fact properly warmed up.

More specifically, ask yourself what breaks you are doing, what movements you'll be making. If you're going to break with a combination of kicks and punches and ridge hands, for example, take yourself briskly through each movement 8–10 times, slowly at first, then gradually adding more power.

Before you perform your actual break, you should be aware of every muscle group involved. Each group should be carefully stretched and warmed before you get down to business.

Pu Gill Gwon, a Tae Kwon Do master whose breaks include a showy strike that takes the top off whiskey bottles without spilling the contents, toppling the bottle, or cutting his hand, warms up prior to a breaking demonstration by pounding his fists against concrete with gradually increasing force, making sure thereby that he is striking with a properly made fist and reducing the subsequent shock levels experienced on contact with his materials.

Deep Breathing

Other breaking experts such as *Washin-Ryu* karate master Hidy Ochiai supplement their warm-ups prior to breaking with a few seconds of deep breathing. Whether or not you perform the *sanchin kata*—Ochiai looks to that kata as the source of his own considerable physical strength—you may derive some benefit from deep breathing.

Inhale deeply through your nose, envisioning as you do so that you are pushing the air down to your center of gravity, or *hara*. Hold your breath momentarily, then exhale entirely through your mouth. Whatever such breathing does or doesn't do for your *ki* power, my guess is you'll find it definitely clears the mind and helps your concentration.

Takayuki Kubota.

8
BREAKING MATERIAL AND SPEED BREAKING

For many years and for a variety of reasons, wood has been the material of choice for martial artists demonstrating breaking skills. But there are some woods you should never try. Forget about hardwoods unless your father is an orthopedist and you want to hurt yourself. Likewise commercial paneling or plywood. In fact, begin at the beginning.

Number one grain white pine is probably the easiest, most breakable commercially available wood. You pay for it by the board foot, and your local lumberyard will cut it to your specifications for an added nominal cost.

The best approach is to choose the wood yourself. You want boards in which the grain is faint and straight. Avoid pieces of wood with dark, closely spaced, or uneven grain patterns; they're going to be harder to break because you won't be working entirely with the grain. Twelve-inch lengths of $1'' \times 10''$ pine are probably ideal. (The 1 refers to the boards' thickness, the 10 to its width. These, like all such measurements, are approximate. The 1-inch thicknesses are more likely to be about ¾ or ⅝ of an inch thick.)

Knots can be a problem, as anyone who's ever tried to saw through one can tell you. On the other hand, the knot weakens the board surrounding it, so a break a few inches to the side of a knot will probably be a little easier. Also, inspect the wood for warp. If it's bent, you won't be able to strike it just right; you may fail to break the board or you may injure yourself.

Dryness makes the wood brittle, and brittleness obviously is going to make the wood easier to break. Therefore, choose high-grade wood that has been stored indoors. If you want to give yourself a little extra breaking edge, you can probably arrange some way to bake your wood a little before your actual demonstration by acquiring it a few days in advance. Beware, however, of fires that might result from such "brainstorms" as putting it in the oven. You can safely place boards in a sunny, but dry room.

Red and yellow pine and redwoods can also be broken by more experienced breakers. But red and yellow pines are unpredictably hard and tough-grained, and redwood is dangerously splintery.

It's probably best to stick with white pine and just add to the number of pieces you break as your skill level rises. You can also add more techniques, executing some breaks with side kicks, others with backfists, knifehands, and front kicks.

Remember, while people in the audience may be impressed by the thickness of your materials and the amounts of it you break, the savvy martial artists watching you are going to be looking at your materials to try to guess how you've cheated or to try to evaluate the quality of your techniques.

Among the educated, breaks done with crisp technique are much preferred to sloppy though powerful blows and heaps of cement and ice on the floor.

BREAKING BRICKS AND TILES

Lumberyards and building supply warehouses stock a wealth of different materials under the category of bricks and tiles—everything from the usual 3½″ × 7½″ × 2¼″ to 16″ square patio tiles, to the curved tiles so favored in California and Mediterranean styles of architecture and the ash-gray cinder block, those mainstays of industrial buildings everywhere.

All of these come in a bewildering number of grades, sizes, costs, and degrees of hardness.

Ed Brown and Tak Kubota favor the breaking of the hardest possible bricks. For these they choose what are called *chimney bricks.* Chimney bricks are just that, bricks used in the construction of chimneys. Since they are subjected to the considerable heat of fireplaces, these bricks are fired, or baked, at extremely high temperatures. They are very hard.

Ed Brown says you can tell the brick's hardness by jabbing at it with the edge of a coin or by dropping a quarter on it: "The more it gives off a musical-type note, the harder it is and the harder it's going to be to break. The flatter it sounds, the softer the material."

In the main, materials that are fired at higher temperatures will be more difficult. But also, you need to consider the ratio of cement to gravel in various grades of lesser brick or cinder block. Make it easy on yourself. Talk to the employees of the yard where you're buying the bricks or cinder blocks. In general, the cheaper stuff will present you with fewer problems. Another good test is to buy one of several kinds you may be thinking of breaking, take the bricks or tiles

home, and whack them with a heavy hammer. The ones that break most easily under your hammer blows will also break more easily with hands and feet.

Bricks, tiles, and cinder blocks are harder to break than wood in that students generally cannot hold them steady enough. Another problem with breaking these strong materials has to do with placement. You need a strong base of support. If you try to break bricks by placing them on cinder block bases, you may break the cinder blocks without so much as cracking the bricks. Many breakers of brick use special metal tables or anvils.

Remember that the closer your bricks or other materials are to the floor, the harder it will be to hit them with the necessary force to go through them. Height and placement of your materials is extremely important.

BREAKING ICE

Years ago, a friend from France was commenting on the American diet. "Your desserts are so big," he said. "They are bigger than the main courses often. I think in America the love affair with volume for volume's sake may go on forever."

Ice is the volume lover's breaking material. Those who are convinced that a 10-ounce slice of pie will be better than a 3-ounce slice are also more likely to be impressed with a break that divides huge slabs of ice. Ice in the big slabs favored by martial artists can be bought (sometimes delivery is free) at any number of restaurant or liquor store supply companies.

Unfortunately, the breaking of ice has become somewhat discredited in recent years. There are many ways to cheat at a break like this, from layering it inside with salt to having it delivered prescored by tools. Certain showmen seem to have made a game out of stacking slabs of ice thicker than human bodies into gigantic towers and then straining the credibility of their audiences by breaking through five or six slabs with an elbow strike or a forearm smash.

Don't get me wrong. There are legitimate martial artists who break structurally sound blocks of ice, but aside from the mess it inevitably makes on the floor—mops and brooms never quite do the cleanup tasks needed—ice breaking techniques lack a kind of finesse. Heads, elbows, and forearms have their place in the martial arts. But you don't really have to know karate to use these weapons effectively. My guess is that, pound for pound, truck drivers or teamsters could break as much ice with elbows, heads, and forearms as black belts. But let's see the teamster's local break boards in midair with flying side kicks like Hee Il Cho or bricks with bare knuckles like Tak Kubota!

So, do you want a 16-ounce slab of doughy apple pie from Terry's truckstop or a 3-ounce sliver of torte made from the very finest ingredients? Whom do you hope to impress?

SHOULD YOU BREAK GLASS?

Several years ago Evel Knievel tried to ride a jet-propelled motorcycle over the Grand Canyon. Naturally, he didn't make it. To me, his jump was to motorcycling what the breaking of glass panes is to martial arts. Likewise, fire breaks. They are theatrical, showy, and dangerous, but there is some question about whether or not they demonstrate any martial prowess beyond what could be demonstrated by the breaking of boards or bricks.

Nearly seven years of experience at tournaments and demos—not to mention the indirect experience of reading manuscripts, proposals, and reports—leads me to conclude that while breaking glass often requires less power and skill than other materials it also leads to a disproportionate number of breaking-related injuries.

Reckless warriors often lead the shortest lives. They are so intent on proving their courage that they jump at the first opportunity to do so and often throw their lives away without regard to any other concern than proving their bravery. Many martial artists believe it's an embarrassment to the martial arts to see someone risk future well-being and give his blood for the sake of entertaining an audience.

While there is certainly nothing wrong with demonstrating and promoting the martial arts, it would seem that demonstrations in which people slice hands and elbows to the bone do as much to injure the arts as about anything else. How much better to take a few moments to educate the audience, explaining that it requires better technique to break safer materials!

SPEED BREAKING

Many people in the martial arts have become less than enthusiastic and even fairly cynical about the value of breaking. This undoubtedly stems from a general weariness in the martial arts with showmanship for the sake of showmanship. It is also a reaction to the less than honest breaking demonstrations experienced martial artists have seen over the years. There are a thousand ways to cheat on a break—from having the boards sawed partly through, to layering the inside of an ice block with salt, to using only the lowest-grade brick or cinder block (inclined to crumble when dropped only the shortest distance). Nevertheless, most good black belts are impressed with difficult feats or breaks they know are honest. Hee Il Cho, for instance, often demonstrates an ability to break boards that have been thrown in the air. Speed breaks like this are all but impossible to fake, a fact that goes a long way toward explaining why Cho's breaking skills are so respected in the martial arts world.

To train for such speed breaks you will want to do more than condition your hands and feet on the *makiwara* and heavy bags. You will need to learn to strike with speed, skill, and a nearly flawless sense of timing. Therefore, you will need to develop and calibrate your progress toward this goal by learning to strike moving targets.

Speed bags of the type that are suspended between the floor and ceiling by elasticized cords are quite useful in this respect. To consistently strike a speed bag as it whips back and forth toward you takes more than a little timing and accuracy. At first, it takes some effort just to make contact every second or third time the bag whips back toward you. As you improve your timing, you can switch hands and strikes, learning to anticipate the bag's responses accurately. The standard boxer's punching bag, hooked to an overhead board and struck every third time it returns, is only slightly less useful in this regard.

For developing speed there are a very wide variety of focus pads, mitts, and targets available through martial arts stores. If you want to specialize in speed breaking, you'll need to have quick partners move the pads in and out of your striking range. Also, smaller pads can be tossed across kicking or punching range until you begin to develop the all-important timing.

SPEED-BREAKING DRILL: In order to learn how to time your punch to strike falling boards or moving objects, you'll need to practice an explosive forward movement. **Using a small pad and a mobile partner, the model is able to practice delivering power to padded objects in motion.**

As you learn to hit moving targets, you'll need to add power as you can. You'll find that when you're breaking a moving target you need something extra in the way of snap and power.

Learning to do speed breaks has obvious advantages over the more or less standard breaks. After all, outside the confines of your demonstration, you can bet most of your human targets are going to be moving rapidly in and out of range.

9
GALLERY OF BREAKERS

TAKAYUKI KUBOTA: IRON HANDS AND HAPPY LAUGHTER

Though there are many accomplished black belt martial artists with breaking skills, there are a few whose skills and attitudes have brought them recognition outside their respective regions. In spite of space limitations we've included here representatives from Japanese, Korean, and Chinese martial arts, from the West, Midwest and East Coasts. Here then are the thoughts and viewpoints of some of the best breakers in the United States.

Shihan Takayuki Kubota threw his first reverse punch somewhere around the age of four in Kumamoto, Japan. Now, more than 40 years later, he's still at it. And while it's a long way from prewar Japan to Glendale, California, watching Kubota move through his karate techniques, you can see how his boyhood love has matured into a uniquely satisfying way of life. In addition to his eighth-degree black belt in his style of *Gosoku-Ryu* karate, Kubota has acquired black belts in judo, aikido, and kendo. Sound like a born fighter? Maybe; but you'd hardly expect a fighter to spend so much time laughing and joking.

Never mind the years and years he's pounded his hands and feet and elbows and knees into mallets on the *makiwara* board or the fact that at 5'4" he's taught police departments in Japan and Los Angeles (where he currently instructs police self-defense instructors in handcuffing and baton techniques). We're talking about somebody who jokes with fry cooks and busboys, pounds his hands and feet with a 12-pound sledgehammer, and spars with his seven-year-old students on his hands and knees. He likes nothing better than showing visitors the six-inch plastic peg he's attached to key chains and patented as the Kubotan (a handy mini-weapon to have in a dark parking lot). And with the slightest encouragement he'll show you the knees and elbows and sweeps he teaches cops to apply so they can get the cuffs on a suspect. Or he'll put his thickened, hard hands down on the table for you and show you how he's reshaped them over the years. He'll tell you he's taught champions like the late John Gehlson, Chuck Norris's rival Tonny Tulleners, and the gigantic Val Mijailovic. If there's still a little more time to talk, he'll tell you about his sideline: appearances in movies and television. Maybe he hasn't appeared in more spots than anyone else in the martial arts. But it seems that way. Sir John

Old and faded though this photo of Shihan Tak Kubota is, it illustrates very clearly the kind of absolute commitment necessary to a successful break. This photo was taken in Japan, probably in the late fifties.

Gielgud he's not. But then there's no better cinematic barbarian/clown anywhere. He's started more movie fights than boy scouts have started campfires—Chinese, Japanese, Eskimo, American Indian, and, with a little makeup, Greek or Italian. He likes to get his acting work out of the way in the morning, though. That way, he can be back in his *dojo* for the afternoon classes. After 45 years, he still can't get enough karate.

Shihan Kubota began conditioning his hands and feet in Japan after the war. "The old-style *makiwara* was made of rough hemp rope," he says. "It scraped wherever you hit. And even though you're hitting with the first two knuckles, all of the knuckles automatically became hard."

He stresses that breaking is only a kind of testing and that, without a martial arts context, it is quite meaningless. He did not, he is quick to point out, train to break boards and bricks, but toughened his entire body with the goal of becoming a complete martial artist. "Conditioning the hands and feet," he says, "should not become a goal in itself."

While he believes that the *makiwara* and heavy bags are ideal training devices, he recommends toughening the feet and hands by kicking and punching in the sand at the beach.

Not only can Shihan Kubota break with spear hands and other comparatively difficult techniques; when he breaks with a roundhouse kick,

In another old photo, Tak Kubota demonstrates karate power for a group of American wrestlers visiting Japan—5'4" can be powerful, too.

At a tournament in America in what looks to be about 1964, Kubota impresses spectators with his powerful hammerfist.

his big toes are doing the damage (most martial artists break with the ball of the foot in such a kick). He has strengthened his toes, he explains, by doing leg raises up on his tiptoes (way up) with as much as 200 pounds of weight across his shoulders.

He has spared almost no surface of his body from the rigors of *makiwara* training. This makes his karate particularly lethal. "It's not necessary to block techniques," he says, "unless you can hurt your opponent when you block."

The *makiwara,* he explains, is extremely useful when it comes to lessons about ideal striking distances. "There are many different kinds of punches," he explains. "Many of them are ignored by people today. But by punching the *makiwara,* you can tell the proper distance of the underhand punch—all the different kinds of punches. The *makiwara* will show you where your punches are too long or too short. That way you will learn to throw the best punch to accomplish the most damage to your opponent."

JOKO NINOMIYA: REMEMBERING TO KEEP FIRST THINGS FIRST

Street fight karate—that's the way Joko Ninomiya presents his karate school to passersby in Denver, Colorado. It sounds like an open invitation. And in some ways it may be. Still, that is the type of karate that most interests the Ashihara karate black belt.

Born 30 years ago in Japan, Ninomiya trained there under Kancho Kideyuki Ashihara until receiving permission from his style's master and namesake to import this rough-and-tumble karate style to America. Ninomiya, at the time he arrived in New York, was about 19. Already he'd placed eighth in the All Japan Open Karate tournament, and though he was living in New York, he journeyed back to Japan to compete for several more years—each time to fight against the best Japan had to offer. In 1976, he lost the tournament by one point, taking second place. But the following year, at 23, he finally captured

Here Shihan Joko Ninomiya demonstrates his shin break of two regulation baseball bats taped together. Note the very carefully arranged bracing of the bat and compare this to the photo of Ninomiya toughening his shin on the rubber-tired *makiwara* in his yard (Chapter 7).

the championship that had been eluding him.

Meanwhile, back in the States, he saw greater personal opportunities for himself west of the Mississippi, eventually traveling to Denver, Colorado, with little more than his *gi* and his black belt. Unable at first to rent a place to begin his teaching, Ninomiya began teaching a small group of enthusiasts in Denver's Cheesman Park. After a struggle to find a suitable school, Ninomiya finally set up shop in his present location, free at last to teach his no-frills karate.

The hard Ashihara style is derived from the *Kyokushinkai* style originally developed by Mas Oyama. At his school, Ninomiya doesn't teach *kata,* for instance, but works almost exclusively in controlled sparring techniques and angling. He teaches his students to stay back out of the

way and to angle off until they can finally assume the offensive. When they do assume the offensive it's invariably a case of preferring the lower, plainer, and harder techniques—elbows, knees, sweeps, and stomps. And, with his toughened legs and shins, Ninomiya displays little hesitation about sharply kicking the legs of fighters daring to attack with kicks of their own.

Each spring Ninomiya hosts a tournament that requires contestants to break boards before every match. At this event, Ninomiya often feels called upon to demonstrate that he is not asking students to do what he himself could not. What better way to demonstrate this than by taping two baseball bats together and breaking them with a shin?

"I started breaking when I was about 16. The first thing I broke was roof or *kawara* tiles. In those days we conditioned our hands and feet on the *makiwara* and on heavy bags filled with sand."

Like Tak Kubota, Ninomiya stresses that breaking is not all there is to karate. "Karate,"

Text continues on page 63.

Here Ninomiya powers through four pine boards with an elbow smash. Note the position of the left hand, intended to shield his face from chunks of board.

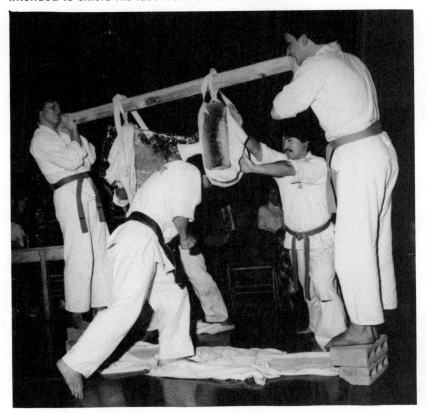

Having rigged a 100-pound block of ice with *gi* bottoms, karate belts, and 2×4s, Ninomiya smashes through it with his head. Note the toweling on the floor and the two students behind the block.

Here Joko Ninomiya powers through stacks of ice with a hammerfist. Note that one of the assistants has had a thought for the well-being of his feet and elected to wear shoes. The more than one hundred bones in the foot make it particularly susceptible to injuries from falling chunks of brick, ice, or board. Note that the bricks used to divide the ice blocks are toppling and present a hazard.

he says, "is practice, practice all the time. You develop technique and speed, then breaking becomes automatic. Very easy.

"Also, you don't need to hit hard things so much," he explains. "Soft bag, soft surfaces will make the wrists firm. You learn the *tanden* breathing from the deep stomach; these things will be of help."

ED BROWN: A MAN WHO IS A FRIEND OF PAIN

Ed Brown doesn't think experience is the best teacher: he thinks pain is. "I mean," says Brown, warming to his subject, "I like pain. I like to feel pain. No pain, no gain. I broke my foot once in front of 2,000 people by kicking three bricks that were flat on the floor. I broke the bricks, all right, but my foot went right through to the floor. I wasn't thinking right. There was a lot of pain. The arch of my foot was actually going the opposite way. Through pain, you can come to understand that you've just learned something."

Ed Brown has been studying *Isshin-Ryu* karate for 30 years. He started under Jake Eckonrode at Camp Lejeune, North Carolina. Together, both Eckonrode and Brown also trained under the late Tatsuo Shimabuku.

"Breaking always intrigued me," Brown admits. "Being a very small man, I guess I always felt I needed an extra edge. There's something pure about *tameshiwari,* or breaking, because it shows that if you actually get to your opponent, you're going to be able to do damage. Actually, without the *tameshiwari,* most people who aren't involved couldn't understand what karate was about.

"Most people say that learning how to break is no good or that you can break a board but the board's standing still while the man isn't. I understand all that, but it's usually people that can't do it themselves that have something to say about someone else."

Can Brown make other use of his hand and body conditioning? He has reported reaching up and tearing branches off trees in order to give punks an idea of what he could do to them. "I'd rather intimidate a guy than obliterate him," Brown says.

Years of conditioning his hands, feet, and elbows have caused his joints and bones to calcify, to harden and become larger than before. "I've broken over 112 bones in my body over the years," Brown reports. "One time in breaking with my head I went clean through the bricks and broke my nose."

Does the prospective breaker have to be prepared to face this sort of ongoing agony?

"He has to be prepared to accept blood, sweat, and tears," Brown replies. "But he should only do this kind of training under a bona fide instructor." Kichiro Shimabuku, current head of the *Isshin-Ryu* style of karate, used to do a lot of breaking, according to Brown, but "his fingers went numb and he couldn't type with them anymore."

Brown will admit that he, too, has lost some feeling in his hand. "Yes, when I write, after about 5 or 10 minutes my writing starts getting sloppy. My hand is better at making rapid movements than being held in the same position all the time. The nerves are a little numbed."

Still, Brown goes on with his almost fanatical training, "hitting against a tree, the point of an anvil, or a very heavy anvil that doesn't move."

Though he used to break with his forehead, Brown says he gave that up in 1975 when Kichiro Shimabuku, the new head of the *Isshin-Ryu* style, informed Brown that a friend of Shimabuku's had developed a blood clot behind his eyes and gone blind. "I think breaking with the head may be dangerous," Brown admits. "Number one, you need a very strong neck."

Brown says he doesn't require his students to engage in breaking, but admits that he strongly encourages it. "It's going to put the razor's edge on your karate," he says.

Describing his own mental attitude, Brown says, "I'm a person of great perseverance. I don't doubt myself. Maybe I won't accomplish it today. For example, I flunked my first black belt test. And yet today I think I'm better than the average karate instructor. I flunked my first driving test. I flunked my first hunting test. Now every year we go hunting. I was eventually on the Marine Corps Rifle Team. When something did defeat me the first time, I always got ready so it couldn't do it again. See, the problem with Americans is that they have to see somebody else do it first. My philosophy is more like an Oriental's. I don't know if it can be done, but I'm going to try it until I can do it."

Here Professor Ed Brown shows a pair of fists heavily calcified and callused from many years of conditioning and breaking.

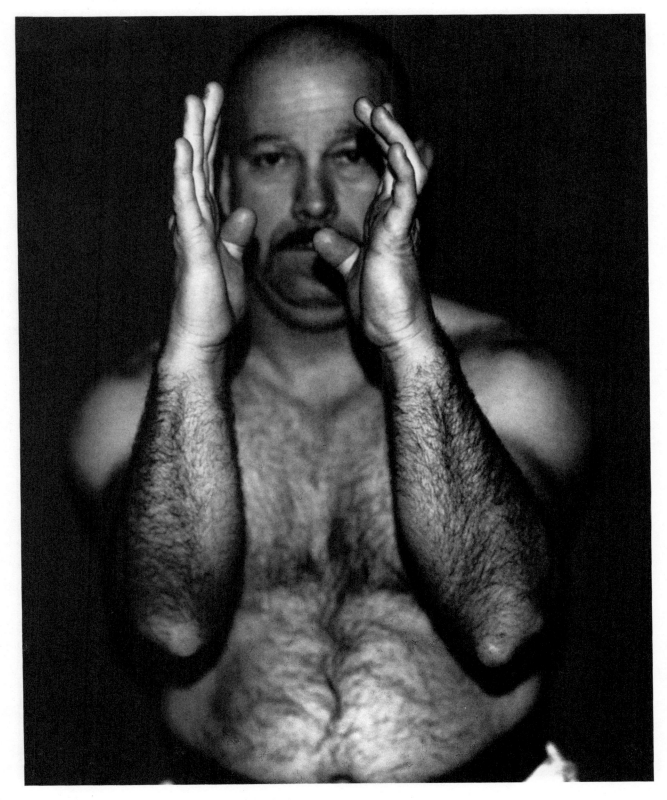

The edge of Brown's left hand is considerably larger
than that of his right. He conditions mainly his left
hand.

As with other masters of breaking, Brown stresses
there's more to the martial arts than breaking. Here,
he demonstrates how his hardened elbow and knee
would hurt his attacker.

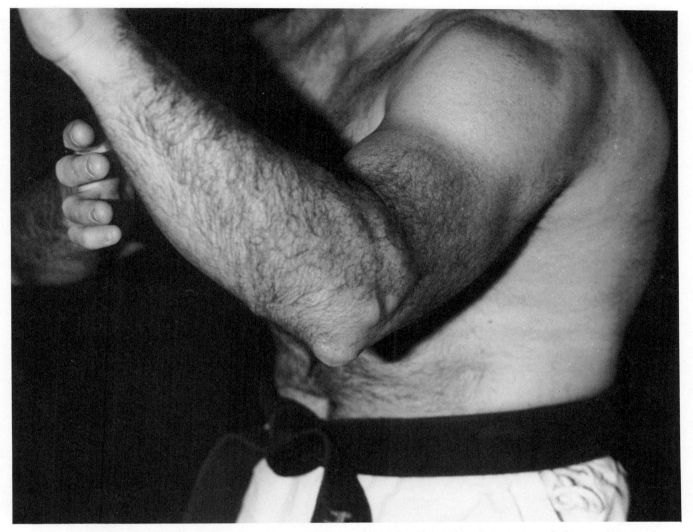

This is the elbow that has beat on trees, _makiwara_ boards, and even anvils. The bump is composed of hardened calcium and bone chips.

RICHARD VERA: THE IRON PALM OF KUNG FU

Many years ago, a kung fu master in Los Angeles named Ark Wong rebelled against age-old racist attitudes and became the first teacher to admit non-Chinese and even non-Asians to his Chinatown Kung Fu Kwoon. Among his first Hispanic students in Los Angeles was Richard Vera, a man who now, 17 years after commencing his training, has been given the reponsibility for passing on Wong's many years of kung fu knowledge.

Vera teaches the Southern 5 Animal system, the Northern _Shaolin_ system, and Northern Pray-ing Mantis styles. As a part of these systems, to a very carefully selected group, he also teaches what he calls "the iron palm technique."

While Vera condedes that the iron palm is a part of many kung fu systems, and that some styles are better at teaching it than others, he himself will instruct only select students in this esoteric yet fascinating aspect of the martial arts. "Students will often ask me, but I feel I must follow the ways of my teacher, Master Wong, and select only those with a good character."

Vera lives the arts. He's a true martial arts fanatic who literally lives in his school and keeps his classes strictly segregated according to train-ing levels. He considers training in iron palm a very serious matter.

"For one thing, you have to follow a certain diet," he explains. "Not only that; there is a period of sexual abstinence. Also, there are

Here Brown breaks two extremely hard chimney bricks with a vertical punch.

Trees have many industrial uses and many martial arts uses. Here Brown smashes the back of his left hand against a tree to condition himself to hitting hard things.

certain changes you have to be prepared for. For instance, once you've started the training, it's difficult to go backward. You can't usually hold an infant in your hands, because the iron palm is a negative *kung*. That means it draws strength from whatever you hold. A baby could die if I held it too long. There are other effects as well. For instance, I'm an aircraft mechanic, and at work I'm known as somebody who's likely to break bolts. Sometimes I twist them right off."

One aspect of the iron palm training consists of rubbing the hands with Tit Tah Jue, a Chinese medicinal mixture that Vera has specially made in Chinatown in Los Angeles, which is said to contain "more than 27 different herbs, minerals,

and live things." Though Vera cautions that this medicine is not for internal consumption—drinking—he admits that some students training in the iron palm have imbibed without apparent harm, even describing its effects as "invigorating."

Vera declined to be specific about many aspects of the iron palm training, offering a sense of personal responsibility as his reason. There are aspects of the training, he explains, that are very specific. According to Vera, students who have gone against certain principles laid down by the masters of the iron palm have become sick and suffered various side effects, ranging from discomfort to serious failures of kidney and liver. "It would be a violation of promises I've made to my teacher to give away information that could prove dangerous to people who just

Text concludes on page 73.

To create hardness in a precise spot, Brown drives
his striking hand repeatedly into a concrete block.

Iron palm expert Richard Vera demonstrates a brick break for a group of his students and friends. Here he demonstrates penetration by breaking the bottom one and sparing the top four.

Slapping a brick can't feel much harder to Vera than the 45-pound bag of lead pellets he conditions his hands on. Here he singles out the top and bottom brick.

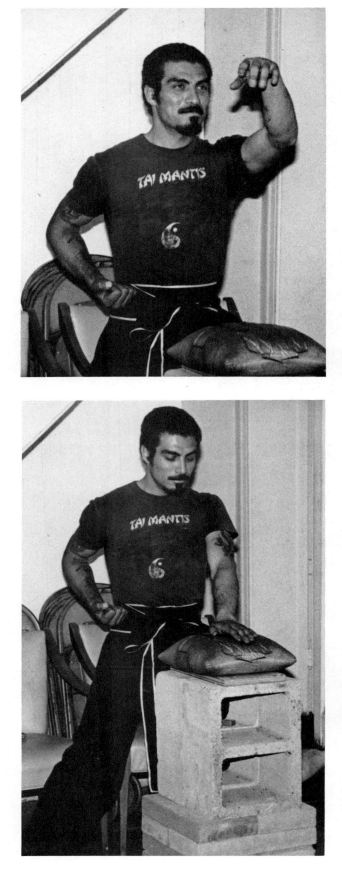

This bag, weighing about 45 pounds and filled with lead pellets, could be said to be the kung fu equivalent of the *makiwara* board. Here, Richard Vera lifts his hand about head high and brings it sharply down. He also conditions the backs of his hands and the fingertips using the same methods.

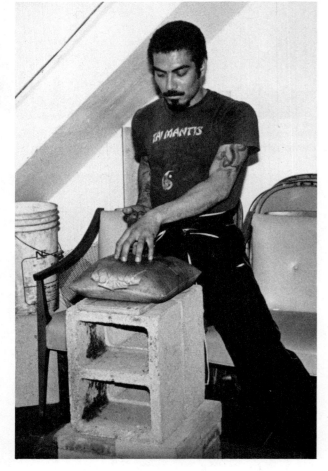

want to try things," he said. "The iron palm technique must be learned in a very carefully supervised environment."

Generally speaking, the iron palm student learns how to coordinate his breath with a slapping and striking routine. Interestingly, while the object of conditioning in the karate arts is to make the striking surfaces hard by creating calluses and calcification, the idea in iron palm training is to avoid creating such a condition and, instead of making the hand hard, to make it heavy.

"The hand is made heavy," Vera explains, "through the concentration of *chi*. Though again I can't be specific, I can say that this is accomplished through what we call *Nui Gung internal power*. Basically, what we're talking about is learning to meditate on a picture in your mind and concentrating on sending all your energy to what we call the *tanten*, the center of us all. The best way I can describe it is like a battery. You learn how to draw the energy in and then, later, to radiate it outward.

"When you've learned to radiate this energy outward and to control it, you can develop a very powerful destructive force. But on the other hand, I've learned that *chi* is also a healing energy. I'm learning to heal my students when they are injured. This, too, is a use of *chi*."

Among the exercises Vera and his iron palm students go through is a routine whereby students clasp and rub together small bundles of chopsticks. Over a long period of time, Vera says the cumulative effect of rubbing the chopsticks together—until they are smooth—combined with breathing exercises will stimulate the flow of *chi* through the shoulder, arm, and hands.

Vera says that, while older masters trained one hand only, he has trained both hands and encourages his students to do likewise. As the training progresses, Vera says, the student can choose for himself whether he wishes to perfect the simple palm slap, the backhand slap, the cut (*shuto*), the spear hand, or the poke (a claw posture resembling the paw of a leopard).

While Vera's iron palm students spend considerable time slapping the heavy bag, he himself works out on a 45-pound canvas sack filled with lead pellets and protected with duct tape. Indeed, when he begins to methodically drop his right hand onto the bag someone entering the school might think he was in a shooting gallery. The slaps sound like gunshots, so much so that Vera often wears earplugs when working out alone.

Penetration rather than raw power being desirable, Vera says he can single out bricks in a high stack, slap the top brick, and break any he chooses; for example, only the 6th and the 9th in a stack of 12.

Though much of what this kung fu teacher claims with respect to *chi* and iron palm training can't be verified by the uninitiated, there are some things easier for an outsider to establish. No question, Richard Vera's hands are large and muscular. They are heavy rather than hardened, and he takes particular pride in the fact that he has not lost any feeling in his conditioned hands. The gunshot reports of his slaps and his effect on the heavy bag when he strikes it indicate that a carefully trained and opened hand can be a potentially lethal weapon.

"The *Nui Gung* internal power system involves more than destruction," Vera explains. "It is a spiritual path. To take this path involves more than just going down and working out."

INDEX